WHAT
YOU NEED TO
KNOW ABOUT
ISLAM
&
MUSLIMS

WHAT YOU NEED TO KNOW ABOUT ISLAM & MUSLIMS

GEORGE W. BRASWELL JR.

BROADMAN
&HOLMAN
PUBLISHERS

Nashville, Tennessee

0–8054–1829–6

Published by Broadman & Holman Publishers, Nashville, Tennessee
Acquisitions and Development Editor: Leonard G. Goss
Page Design and Typesetting: TF Designs, Mt. Juliet, Tennessee

Dewey Decimal Classification: 220
Subject Heading: RELIGION

Unless otherwise noted, Scripture quotations are from the Holy Bible,
New International Version, © copyright 1973, 1978, 1984.
Other versions are marked NASB, the New American Standard
Bible, © Copyright The Lockman Foundation, 1960, 1962, 1963, 1968,
1971, 1972, 1973, 1975, 1977, 1995;
NKJV, New King James Version, copyright © 1979, 1980, 1982,
Thomas Nelson, Inc., Publishers.

Library of Congress Cataloging-in-Publication Data

Braswell, George W.
   What you need to know about Islam and Muslims / George W.
Braswell, Jr.
      p   cm.
   ISBN 0–8054–1829–6 (pbk.)
      1. Islam—Doctrines. 2. Islam—Controversial literature. 3.
Islam—Relations—Christianity. 4. Christianity and other
religions—Islam. I. Title.
   BP161.2 .B733 2000
   297—dc21   99–048857
                                                                    CIP

1 2 3 4 5 04 03 02 01 00

CONTENTS

Contents

Contents

Contents

PREFACE

When I was in high school and college in the 1950s, the religion Islam and the people called Muslims were relatively unknown. Scholars wrote books on Muhammadanism, and Muslims were viewed as tribal peoples in the deserts of Arabia.

In the 1960s when my family and I journeyed to Iran as the first Southern Baptist missionaries appointed by the mission board to this country 99 percent Muslim, I learned deeply of that part of the Islamic world. Muhammad and Mecca, ayatollahs and the Quran, haj and jihad were everyday expressions. I visited in hundreds of Muslim homes and mosques and received great hospitality.

However, Muslims wondered why everyone, including me, had not accepted Islam and become a Muslim. Jesus was a renowned prophet to them but not the Savior. When some Muslims did make a decision to follow Jesus, they led not only a changed life but often one of danger because they had left their mother religion.

In the 1970s, when I joined the faculty of Southeastern Baptist Theological Seminary, Islam was emerging as a growing and powerful global religion. Little had changed in hundreds of years of Christianity's basic ignorance of Islam and outreach to Muslims or of Islam's view of Christianity as a polytheistic and corrupting religion.

In the meanwhile, Islam has soared to over one billion followers with particular mission sights on the Western world of Europe and the United States. And recently, some churches and their mission agencies have become aware of the ever-expanding challenge of Islam and have begun to place more mission resources to encounter the Muslim world in missions, evangelism, and the planting of churches.

This book is written to provide primary information on Islam, its challenges to the Western world and Christian communities, the differences between Islam and Christianity, and the ways of Christian outreach to Muslims. It concludes with a chapter on Muslims in the United States, where their advance is noticeable and powerful, emerging as the second largest religion.

Differences between the major beliefs of Christians and Muslims are real. Muslims are unyielding in their denials of Christian beliefs in the divinity of Jesus, His crucifixion upon the cross, and His resurrection from the tomb. They condemn the Trinity. Christians are unyielding in their unacceptance of Muhammad as the last prophet and of the Quran as the final revelation of God.

In spite of the differences, even beyond them and around them, Christians are called upon by their biblical faith and spiritual sensitivities to reach out to Muslims in love, in service, in speaking the truth with compassion, and in sharing the meaning of their salvation experience in Jesus Christ. Little good has ever been experienced in argumentation, and much less ridiculing and degrading Islam.

What is new and challenging is the nearness and close proximity of Christians to Muslims, particularly in the Western world. There are more fresh opportunities for Christian encounters with Muslims and witness to them. And in spite of the differences, Muslims do believe their Quran when it says that Jesus is the Word and Spirit of God. What does that mean for them? What can the Christian do to help them understand the meanings from the biblical faith? Where there is love, there is hope. The Muslims are here. The Christians are coming.

CHAPTER 1

THE MUSLIMS ARE COMING!

DID YOU KNOW?

The non-Muslim world knows little of the people called Muslims and their religion, Islam. Many people think all Muslims speak Arabic, live in the Middle East, and launch attacks against the state of Israel. In fact, most Muslims live outside the Middle East, speak little if any Arabic, and live normal, peaceful lives.

Muslims who take their religion seriously believe it is the proper and correct religion for all the world. They believe the non-Muslim world is weak and corrupt. It needs Islam. Therefore, Islam should be carried to the ends of the earth. Consider the following:

- There are as many Muslims in Indonesia, the largest populated Muslim nation, as there are Arab Muslims in the heartland of the Middle East.
- Islam has challenged Judaism as the second largest religion in the United States.
- Islam is the second-largest religion in Europe.
- A Muslim leader has inaugurated a session of the United States Senate, praying in the name of Allah.
- The majority of Iranians are Shiite Muslims who expect the return of the twelfth Imam to bring a pure reign on earth.

1

- The third-holiest city for Muslims is Jerusalem, where it is said their prophet Muhammad once ascended to heaven from the Dome of the Rock and spoke with Jesus.

- Every Muslim is on jihad to please God and to spread the true religion Islam.

- The prophet Muhammad was a "warrior king" leading his forces into battles against other tribes, including Jews. In one battle, his forces slaughtered eight hundred male Jews and took their wives and children as booty.

- Some Muslim groups are so militant that they kill civilians in the name of Allah and claim immediate entry to heaven as martyrs.

- Some popular forms of Islam venerate saints and offer prayers to them.

- Muhammad was given a special revelation to have some thirteen wives or concubines, whereas other men could have only up to four wives with certain responsibilities. Muhammad's favorite wife was Aisha; he was betrothed to her when she was six and consummated the marriage when she was nine.

- Islam is one of the fastest-growing world religions, numbering over one billion adherents.

- Saudi Arabia considers itself the caretaker of Mecca, Islam's holiest city, and allows no Christian missionaries to enter it and no Christian churches to be built on its soil. Saudi Arabia spends tens of millions of dollars funding Muslim missionaries and building mosques in countries around the world, including the United States.

- Muslims are a majority in forty-five African and Asian countries.

- One hundred million Muslims live in India, where most inhabitants are Hindus. Almost as many Muslims live in India as in Iran and Egypt combined.

- Of the ten nations with the largest Muslim populations, Muslims are a minority in three—India, China, and Nigeria.

- Muslims are required to pray five times daily facing the city of Mecca.

- Many Muslims think that Christians believe in three deities: God, Jesus, and the virgin Mary.

- Muslim leaders often censure Western nations—especially Europe and the United States—because of their violence, moral corruption, and rampant sexual immorality.

- A United Nations demographic report forecasts Muslims will represent at least half of the global birthrate after the year 2055.

🕮 Saudi Arabia has given tens of millions of dollars to Harvard University and the University of Arkansas to fund Islamic study centers.

🕮 Muslims and Christians in recent times have fought each other in Lebanon, Sudan, Indonesia, and Yugoslavia. These peoples are often restless toward each other in the Middle East, Africa, Asia, and Europe.

THE MUSLIMS ARE COMING . . . THEY ARE HERE!

Muslims have emerged from the desert sands as a growing and powerful religious force. They number over one billion. *Islam* means "submission to God," and *Muslim* means "one who submits to God." Muslims believe that Allah is the only true God and that the Quran, the perfect holy book, teaches the correct way of belief and practice. They believe Islam is a universal and uniform religion for all peoples and cultures with little variety and diversity in its major beliefs and practices.

The Muslims are here! For over 1,400 years Islam has expanded far beyond its Middle Eastern origins. Today Muslims are numerous on every continent: Africa boasts 308,660,000; Asia, 778,362,000; Europe, 32,032,000; Latin America, 1,356,000; North America, 5,530,000; and Oceania, 385,000; for a total of 1,126,325,000.[1] Islam is a world religion characterized by missions, mobility, and militancy.

Classical Islam divides the world into two areas: (1) the world of peace, where Islam is practiced and the Quran is observed; (2) the world of warfare and ignorance, dominated by non-Muslims. The mission of Islam is to bring this second world under Islam.

MISSIONS, MOBILITY, MILITANCY

Islam is a religion with missions at its heart. Every Muslim should strive to please Allah and to offer Allah's religion to others. Islam has been able to cross geographical and cultural divides to gain followers and to make certain adaptations to other cultures for its success.

✳Islam is a missionary religion. It is energized by its theocratic world vision and mission. All of life should be subsumed under the laws of Allah: personal life, family life, culture, society, religion, government. The roots of the vision are in the Quran. Therefore, Muslims are under a mandate to establish this vision wherever Islam is present. Muslims are on mission.

Islam is a mobile religion. It can be carried across populations and cultures. Many memorize the Quran, which is no longer than the New Testament, with 114 chapters, or *suras*, in the Arabic language. Islam's origins in a tribal society made its attributes, notably its patriarchal family and polygamy, applicable to African tribes. Muslim traders carried Islam to Indonesia, and it adapted to the cultural layers of Hinduism and animism in Indonesian society. Indonesia has the largest Muslim population of any country. The simplicity of belief and the practice of the pillars of Islam have made it appealing and approachable across cultures.

[Islam is a militant religion. "Jihad" is an important concept. It has two aspects: (1) the Islamic requirements that the individual must practice to be a worthy Muslim; (2) the warfare of the community against infidels and those who attack or resist Islam.] All Muslims are under mandate to practice jihad because they believe that Islam is the correct and perfect religion and that all other religions are inferior. Not only are they to follow the teachings of the Quran, but they are also to emulate the model of their prophet Muhammad, who led his fighting forces into battle to defend Islam and to make Islam dominant. Waging community or national warfare must follow certain rules interpreted and provided by religious leadership.

Thus, Islam as a missionary, mobile, and militant religion has become the fastest-growing religion worldwide. It has become a religious and political force in Europe, has risen to challenge Judaism as the second-largest religion in the United States, has sent missionaries and monies to bring about Islamic revival in the republics of Central Asia, and has continued to expand across Africa.

WHY DO WE HEAR SO MUCH ABOUT ISLAM?

Here are some reasons that Islam has grown and gained so much attention in recent years.

1. Muslim thinkers and writers have reacted vehemently against the encroachments of European and American culture, politics, and national policies upon Muslim nations and populations and have awakened its followers.
2. Formation of the state of Israel has galvanized Muslim nations and peoples against Israel, for the rights of Palestinians, and for the rights of Muslims to the holy places in Jerusalem.
3. Terrorist acts against peoples, planes, buildings, and nations have been launched by groups using the names of Islam, Muslim, and jihad and have been supported by Islamic interests.
4. Oil wealth has helped Muslim governments strengthen Islamic identity, self-confidence, and political power to counteract Western dominance and to fund Islamic advance—notably in Africa, Europe, Central Asia, and North America.

5. The Iranian revolution, which ousted a Western-leaning Shah and established the fundamentalist Islamic Republic of Iran, has inspired and funded many worldwide Islamic movements that underscore the missionary, mobile, and militant aspects of Islam.
6. The demise of the Union of Soviet Socialist Republics opened up Islamic mission advances inspired by native populations of the republics and supported by help from Saudi Arabia, Iran, and Turkey.
7. Hundreds of thousands of Muslims have moved to Europe and the United States; Islam has become a religion of dominant expression in Europe and the emerging second-largest religion in the United States. Many Muslims have become citizens, have married nationals, and are raising their children as Muslims.

ISLAM RESPONDS

*Muslims must Islamicize non-Muslims by persuasion and conversion. Sometimes force has been a method. If non-Muslims do not accept Islam, they must submit to Islamic authority and rule. Islam is over against the non-Muslim world.[2] Early Jewish tribes refused to submit to the prophet Muhammad and hundreds were slaughtered. Jews have been tolerated with limited freedoms in dominant Muslim territories.

From its very beginning Islam viewed Christianity as a religion of idolatry and contamination. One of the greatest sins—*shirk* in Arabic—is to believe that God could share his nature with humanity. Therefore, Islam denied the Christian beliefs of the Trinity, the divinity of Jesus Christ, the crucifixion and death of Jesus for the sins of the world, and the resurrection of Jesus from the tomb. Through the centuries, Muslims have waged warfare against Christians, both physical and verbal, and Christians have fought Muslims, notably in the Crusades. Where there has been Muslim dominance, Christians have been treated as minorities, *dhimmis*, and given limited freedoms.

Suspicion, distrust, and hostility characterize the history of Christian-Muslim relations. Stereotypes have prevailed. Islam has attacked Christianity for its polytheism and corruption of the Scriptures. Christianity has considered Islam a heretical and impenetrable religion.

The Islamic world has fought the West's impositions of its values, cultural forms, and politics upon Muslim peoples. Accusations of colonialism and imperialism have been heralded especially against Europe and the United States. The Iranian Islamic revolution castigated the United States as the "Great Satan" and cast out Christian missionaries. Saudi Arabia has primarily relied upon the United States for the modernization and technology of its society but prohibits any church or Christian missionary presence on its soil.

Christians, with few exceptions, have maintained their distance from Muslims. They have done little to understand Muslims, to prepare to send missionaries to Muslim people, and to develop a Christian apologetic for Muslims. Christians have continued to be unfamiliar with Muslims and their religion. Mass media has associated the words *ayatollah*, *jihad*, and *terrorist* with Islam. Muslims are stereotyped as warlike, savage, and uncivilized.

Some scholars have written of the coming clash of civilizations between the Islamic world and the Western or Christian world. Christian churches and mission agencies are awakening to the presence and strength of Islam, to its missions worldwide, and to its agenda to become the dominant religious and cultural expression. Christian mission agencies are restructuring their strategies to include the unreached Muslim peoples groups. Christians are discovering that they have Muslim neighbors, that mosques are being built next to churches, that their medical doctors are Muslims, and that their children attend school with Muslims. In the United States a Muslim leader has opened a session of Congress with prayer in the name of Allah. There are Muslim chaplains in the armed services.

The Muslims are coming . . . No! The Muslims are already here. They are worldwide. They are growing in numbers and influence. They offer religious help to millions. They have a religious, social, and political agenda. They present one of the greatest challenges to Christianity and to Christians.

CHRISTIAN RESPONSES TO ISLAM

For over 1,400 years, Islam has considered Christianity to be a false and corrupting religion. Christianity has viewed Islam as a heretical religion. For the most part, each has let the other alone. The present time has brought each other closer. Islam has greatly penetrated the non-Muslim world. Christianity has begun to awaken to the presence of Muslims.

What are Christians and churches to do? Consider the following:

1. Christians should let the past be the past. There has been much ignorance and misunderstanding of Muslims by Christians and vice versa. The past is important for learning and understanding, but Christians and the church must seize the present to prepare for the future.

2. Christians should understand the basics of Islam. Determine the beliefs and practices of what the Quran teaches, of what tradition teaches, of varied interpretations of Muslim thinkers, schools of thought, and ordinary individuals. It is important to know what the Quran teaches about God, Jesus, prayer, judgment, and salvation. It is essential to know what is orthodox Islam and any deviations from it, namely, folk Islam.

3. *Christians should distinguish between different kinds of Muslims.* There are individual Muslims. There are communities of Muslims. Some nations are called Islamic Republics because diverse Muslim peoples live in them. Orthodox Muslims adhere to the letter of the Quran, but folk Muslims mix Islam with tribalism and animism. It is important to know what kind of Islam an individual Muslim observes.

4. *Christians should prepare themselves for Muslims' misunderstandings of Christianity and Christians.* Some Muslims assume that Christians are polytheists, assuming they worship three gods in the Trinity. Some think that every Christian is a Crusader. Christianity is believed to be a warring religion. Some believe that Christians are cannibals in eating the body and blood of Jesus in the Lord's Supper.

5. *Christians should prepare themselves to witness to Muslims.* Christian witness to Muslims is based not only on understanding as much as possible about Muslim belief and practice but also on one's own preparation in Scripture and prayer. One would not invite Muslims to one's table and serve pork. That would be offensive and insensitive. Christians should know that the Quran states that Jesus is messiah, word of God, spirit of God, prophet of God, born of the virgin Mary. Some Muslims may not know the Quran asserts these things, nor do they know the meaning of these ideas, either from the Islamic perspective or from the biblical and Christian perspective. Christians must witness through prayer, understanding, and sensitivity and approach Muslims in knowledge and love. They must give their witness from their own experience in God through relationship with Jesus Christ.

6. *Christians should reach out in witness to Muslims.* Many Muslims and Muslim people groups live in areas of danger from earthquakes, drought, floods, typhoons, and diminished resources. They experience abnormal hunger, poverty, illiteracy, and early death. Christian outreach through the means of food, housing, digging of wells, agricultural training, and literacy in times of need demonstrates Christian love and good will. The Christian gospel may be heard and accepted through deeds and words in critical times. Christians who go in the name of Jesus— "Isa" in Islam—sharing the good news personally and preaching it, may reap the harvest of salvation and reconciliation among Muslims.

7. *Christians should plant churches among Muslim peoples.* For centuries evangelism and church planting among Muslim peoples was slow and nearly nonexistent. New strategies for starting churches have been

initiated. Improved results have been demonstrated. Muslims who seek information about Christianity often place themselves in danger of persecution. Muslims who accept Jesus Christ as their Savior and Lord are often ostracized from their families and communities. Some have been killed.

Muslim people groups have been identified with common language, ethnicity, and similar Islamic roots. These groups may or may not be within national or state boundaries. However, these common traits among Muslims help them to assimilate into a Christian fellowship and church and provide them more security and community. The context of church planting becomes important. Muslim culture becomes critical in terms of what and how a Muslim convert may accommodate and disassociate as one becomes a follower of Jesus in Christian community.

What does the future hold for relations between Christianity and Islam? That is uncertain, but one thing is clear: both religions have a message and a mandate. Christianity has a mandate to go into all the world and preach the gospel, a gospel of salvation and reconciliation in Jesus Christ. Islam has a mandate to practice jihad and to bring the non-Muslim world under the rule of Allah and the injunctions of the Quran.

Scholars may speculate about the clash of civilizations and about accommodations between religions. The mission of the Christian and the church is to present the gospel of love, salvation, and reconciliation to Muslims whose lives may be changed and whose communities may be renewed in Jesus Christ. This book will help you to understand the Islamic world and Muslim peoples and explain how to witness, evangelize, and begin Christian fellowship among them.

CHAPTER 2

MUHAMMAD

Prophet, Ruler, Commander in Chief

A MAN FOR ALL SEASONS

Why begin a study of Islam and Muslims with Muhammad? Because Muhammad founded the religion of Islam. He was a native son of the tribal organization of the Arabian peninsula and the malcontent against the polytheism, animism, and wickedness of the day. He was the visionary who claimed to receive revelations from the supreme God.

Muhammad was the prophet who preached the infallible word of God delivered by the angel Gabriel directly from heaven and written down in the inerrant Quran. It was in the Quran that all the correct beliefs and practices were to be observed.

He was the religious, political, and judicial leader of the Islamic community (umma) which he established and over which he ruled as a king. Through him laws and commandments were announced, interpreted, implemented, and its consequences he judged among the people. Muhammad was the commander in chief of his fighting forces. He planned the warfare. He led his troops into battle. He warred against and killed his fellow tribesmen, the Meccans. He ordered the killing of hundreds of Jews who refused to accept his command and join his community. He divided up the booty and took as wives some whose husbands had been killed in battle.

9

Muhammad was a theocrat. He spoke in the name of God, acted on behalf of God to establish the godly community, and supervised and judged the community's beliefs and actions in order to keep them correct and pure.

Thus Islam was founded by Muhammad (570–632), who had total control over his community and who had all the essentials of a religious-political institution in place by the time of his death. Why start with Muhammad? Two of the greatest authorities for Muslims are the infallible Quran and the example and tradition of Muhammad known as "the hadith." Orthodox Muslims do not worship Muhammad. However, they venerate him, and desire not only to obey the teachings of the Quran but also to emulate the life of their prophet.

FUSSING AND FIGHTING: A RELIGION BORN IN TURMOIL

Religions often begin as a protest or critique against established religions or values or institutions. Often a new religion is viewed as a threat or competition. So Muhammad brought Islam into the seventh century as a new force with significant changes. He was met with resistance and threat of death.

The Arabian peninsula, which includes present-day Saudi Arabia, was populated by various tribes. Nomadic tribes tended herds and cultivated the fields. There were traders and merchants of the towns. Leadership was patriarchal; males were the important lineage. Female babies were often killed. Raiding each other's camps and herds was a form of warfare and competition. Spoils were taken by the leaders for themselves and their warriors. Often women were taken in these raids as booty. Blood revenge was common in warfare.

Swirling around the peninsula were the hostilities between the Persian empire to the east and the Byzantine empire to the west. Persians were Zoroastrians and Byzantines were Eastern Orthodox Christians. Many of the populations in those empires were tired of the warfare and disruptions of life. These dissatisfactions provided an opening for the later advance of Islam. Some peoples were open to try a new religion or to hope for better life under different rulers. The Muslims were to come.

Also, within the Byzantine Empire the Eastern Orthodox Christians had theological differences with the Roman Catholic papacy in Rome. There were disputes over the doctrine of the Trinity and the nature of Jesus Christ. These disputes were later to influence Muhammad and his understanding of Christianity. Islam came to deny the central Christian teachings of the divinity and crucifixion of Jesus, and Jesus as Savior for the sins of humankind.

The preaching of Muhammad also brought crisis to the tribes of the peninsula. The culture of the peninsula included polytheism, animism, and tribal institutions and values. Muhammad, a member of the prestigious Quraish tribe, preached against the gods and goddesses worshiped by his kinfolk and the tribes. He attacked the corrupt practice of killing female infants. At first the tribes ignored him. Then his life was threatened, and he fled.

Thus, within the peninsula and beyond there were conflicts between empires, within Christianity, between tribes, and between Muhammad and his fellow tribesmen. Muhammad established his religion in the midst of much fussing and fighting.

MECCA: THE CITY OF MUHAMMAD AND ALLAH

[The holiest city of Islam is Mecca. Muslims believe it is the place where Abraham was asked to sacrifice Ishmael (not Isaac as told in the Old Testament).] It is the birthplace of Muhammad. All Muslims are commanded in the Quran to make a pilgrimage to Mecca once in a lifetime. Over one billion Muslims are commanded to pray five times daily facing Mecca. Non-Muslims are barred from entering the city.

Marriage to a Wealthy Widow: Visions in a Cave

Muhammad was born into the Quraish tribe in Mecca around 570. His tribesmen were the keepers of the kaba, a place of offerings to various deities of the day. He was reared by his uncle after the early death of his parents. Little is known of his childhood. At age twenty-five he married Khadija, a wealthy widow merchant fifteen years older than he. He led her trade caravans as far away as Damascus.

In his leisure time Muhammad retreated to a cave on Mount Hira, outside Mecca, for relaxation. (In 610, at age forty, he received a vision from the angel Gabriel during the month of Ramadan. The angel told him to recite. Thus began the preaching of Muhammad of this revelation from Allah to the wayward tribes of Mecca.

From 610 to 622, the angel brought more revelations. Over time these were collected and became the Quran. Tradition holds that Muhammad was illiterate and that his followers remembered his preachings and codified them into the Quran by 652, some twenty years after his death.

Tribal Persecution and Escape to Medina

The preaching of Muhammad got him into trouble. He attacked the deities of the kaba and proclaimed Allah as the only God. This attack went to the heart of the religious and commercial interests associated with the kaba and economic interests of the merchants. His own tribe turned against him.

Only a few converted to his preaching in Mecca. These included his wife Khadija, his cousin Ali, Umar an influential tribesman, and his companion Abu Bakr, a distinguished merchant. Ali married Muhammad's daughter Fatima, who gave the prophet two grandsons, Hasan and Husain. His detractors accused him of disseminating information from the Jews and Christians. Some dismissed him as a lunatic and said he needed medical attention.

During this time Muhammad claimed a supernatural experience. He confessed to his wife his fear of being disillusioned by visions. She reassured him of his sanity. Muhammad told the story of his being taken by Gabriel to Jerusalem. On the spot of the present Dome of the Rock, he was taken up into heaven to view it and to meet Abraham, Moses, and Jesus, whom he led in prayer. Later he was returned to Mecca.

In 619, his wife and his uncle died. He married Sawdah, a widow. His tribe refused to protect him. Threats were made against him. Some of his followers fled for protection to the Christian king of Abyssinia. Muhammad had been reminded earlier of the counsel of Khadija's Christian cousin, Waraqa, who had compared him to Moses. He continued to believe strongly that his experiences with the angel Gabriel on Mt. Hira were from Allah.

Mecca was Muhammad's birthplace. It was the place of his visions. His preaching of monotheism found resistance among his own people. He was persecuted. His life and that of his followers were on the verge of extinction. He had to flee. But he was later to return in triumph and establish Mecca as the premier city of Islam. It was to become the city of pilgrimage required of all Muslims. The kaba was to be cleansed of its idols. The great mosque was to be built. Allah was to be submitted to in its holy precincts.

THE FLIGHT TO MEDINA: WARFARE, VICTORY, AND COMMUNITY

Flight in Haste: Key Date in Islam

In the midst of Muhammad's problems, leaders from various tribes came to him from Medina, two hundred miles to the north. They sought his leadership in Medina among the tribes and pledged an oath to obey and fight for him. As the tribes of Mecca plotted to send a young man from each tribe to kill Muhammad, Muhammad sent his followers to Medina, where they were provided protection.

✳ July 16, 622, is the most famous date in Islam. It is known as the flight to Medina, the Hegira. It is the beginning of the Islamic calendar, year 1 A.H. (After the Hegira). Muhammad, Ali, Abu Bakr, and his followers took up residence in what was to become the second most important city in Islam.

Medina, known also as Yathrib, the city of the Prophet, was an agricultural oasis inhabited by warring Jewish and Arab tribes. There was also strife between the emigrant Muslims from Mecca and the helpers or citizens in Medina. Muhammad was sought to settle disputes and bring unity. It was a place for Muhammad to establish his new religion.

Love and Hate: *Wipeout of the Jews*

✳ To appease the Jews, Muhammad proposed Friday as the sabbath and prayer facing Jerusalem five times daily. After many Jews rejected his leadership, Muhammad chose to pray facing Mecca, and he exchanged the Jewish Day of Atonement for the monthlong fasting season of Ramadan.

He adopted Abraham as patriarch, considering him the father of all Arabs as father of Ishmael through whose lineage Muslims claim descent. Abraham became the first and most prominent *hanif*, the obedient one or Muslim.

Muhammad engaged in many battles with his fighting forces. The Jewish tribes were either expelled or executed. In a battle with the last Jewish tribe around Medina, seven to eight hundred men were slaughtered. Women and children became the booty of the Muslim warriors.[1]

Muhammad later married a Jewish widow and a woman from the vanquished tribes. He continued to have high regard for Jewish monotheism, calling Jews "People of the Book." He accepted them as long as they submitted to his authority as leader of the community and did not stand in his way of fighting idolatry and polytheism.

Several battles were engaged with Meccan fighting forces as Muhammad solidified his ruling power in and around Medina. Not until 630 would the Muslim forces take the city of Mecca and establish Islam as the major religion with the kaba as its central worship focus.

Religion and State: *The Community (Umma) of Islam*

During his years in Medina, Muhammad established the foundations for his new religion. He developed a document, the constitution of Medina, which declared the existence of a community of people known as "the umma," who submitted to Allah and to the "last prophet" Muhammad.[2] The prophet's rule was based on the injunctions in the Quran.

Islam sought to answer three questions: how to live correctly, how to think correctly, and how to organize life correctly. The character of the community was structured on religious affiliation rather than on tribal blood kinship. The brotherhood of Islam replaced the brotherhood of the tribes. Allah and Muhammad were the center and reference for the people. Muhammad received directives from Allah as unquestioned directives for the people. Thus the early Muslim community was founded on a theocratic polity.

Idolaters and unbelievers were considered enemies of the Islamic community. The world was divided into two areas: the world of Islam and the world of disobedience. Through struggle and warfare the world of disobedience was to be brought under the authority and subjugation of the world of Islam. Thus Islam was the correct and pure religion, and jihad was the method to bring others into it through conversion or through domination.

Muslims made peace or war. They collected a tax from non-Muslims and provided protection for them. In raiding expeditions a fifth of the booty went to Muhammad for personal and public purposes; his warriors received the rest.

From 622 to 632, Muhammad built his mosque and established the basic beliefs and practices of Islam in Medina. They included rituals of prayer, almsgiving, fasting, and pilgrimage. He continued to receive revelations from Allah and administered religious, economic, political, military, and legal affairs. He was the prophet, statesman, ruler, preacher, warrior, and messenger of Allah without peer or equal.

CAPTURE OF MECCA: MUHAMMAD'S DEATH

On January 1, 630, the prophet led an army of ten thousand against Mecca. Additional warriors joined them on the way to the holy city. Meccans offered little resistance, for many of them had already embraced the new religion. Thus the orphaned man who had eight years earlier left the city in secret and under duress entered triumphantly.

He demanded a pledge of loyalty from every man and woman. He cleansed the kaba of its idols. He cited the injunctions of the Quran for all Muslims to make the pilgrimage to the kaba. He condemned paganism and the veneration of ancestors. He proclaimed that there was no god but Allah and Allah had no associates.

Polytheists were forbidden to enter the holy precincts of the mosque and the kaba. He stated his obligation to use force to convert polytheists to the true worship of Allah. Jews and Christians as believers and "People of the Book" could worship in their traditions, but they had to pay the poll tax and submit to Islamic rulership.

After establishing Islam firmly in Mecca, Muhammad returned to his family, property, and place of rule in Medina. He chose to live the several remaining years in the city which came to be known as al-Medina, the City of the Prophet.

He extended his authority widely throughout the Arabian peninsula north to Aqaba and south to Mecca. Tribes converted to Islam. Others sought his protection by paying taxes. Delegations came to Muhammad from all over Arabia. Syrian and Yemeni traders crossing lands he controlled were required to gain permission and pay taxes.

Muhammad performed his last pilgrimage to Mecca in March of 632. Having returned to Medina, he died in June in the quarters of his favorite wife, Aisha, whom he had married when she was nine years old. The prophet had never made a formal or public announcement about his successor, and succession would prove to be a challenging time for the community. Ultimately, division would occur. Two major groups would emerge vying for leadership—the Sunnis and the Shiites.

LEGACY OF MUHAMMAD

The Supreme Leader

Three principal sources provide information about the life of Muhammad.

- Ishaq, who in 775 wrote a reverential biography of Muhammad in Arabic
- The hadith, a collection of sayings of and stories about Muhammad, evaluated by Islamic authorities upon the reputation of the collectors
- The Quran, which discloses much of the prophet's thought and behavior

At the time of his death, Muhammad had emerged as a religious and political leader without equal in the Arabian peninsula. He had founded a community, in fact a nation, based on a monotheistic and prophetic religion. He had taught and required of his followers an orderly lifestyle of prayer, fasting, and pilgrimage.

The crescent moon was to become the symbol displayed on flags and mosques. The mission of Islam was set to go forth into the wider world. Under his aegis, the world had been divided into two realms: (1) the world of Islam, or submission to Allah and his Quranic commands; and (2) the world of disobedience to Allah or the world of ignorance.

Islam was to subjugate the world of disobedience under its authority through conversion, force, and carefully controlled measures of taxation and submission. After Muhammad's death, Islam moved quickly beyond the peninsula to claim vast territories and populations.

Tradition and Change

The legacy of Muhammad also includes changes which Islam brought to tribal culture. He advocated marriage and family and allowed a plurality of wives. The Quran allowed a man to marry up to four wives if they were all treated with equity. The tribal culture had allowed unlimited wives. Inheritance was to be shared by both men and women. However, men were favored with two shares to every one share for women. A wife could keep the husband's dowry even in divorce.

Before Islam the security of life and property was protected by blood feud and by *lex talionis* of the tribes. Muhammad replaced the tribal concept with the community of Islam. He taught that believers in Allah who deliberately killed other believers would be penalized in hell.

Muhammad accepted existing slavery but called for kind treatment of slaves and their freedom. He disliked the Jewish practice of lending money at interest and prohibited taking interest within the Islamic community.

Muhammad's Assessment of Himself

A tradition has given the prophet's own words about himself and his standing among others:

- Allah made him victorious by frightening his enemies.
- The earth was made for him and for praying.
- Booty was made lawful for him but not lawful for those before him.
- He was given the right of intercession on the day of resurrection.
- Prophets were sent to the nations, but only he was sent to all mankind.[3]

What Others Have Said about Muhammad

Orthodox Islam teaches that Muhammad was the last of the prophets with special charisma and gifts. Popular Islam attributes miracles to him as well as sainthood and even divinity. However, Muhammad condemned the worship of the dead at shrines.

For fourteen hundred years Islam has been associated with the man Muhammad. As there are different views of him within Islam, so there are from outsiders. Martin Luther described Muhammad as a destroyer of the Lord Christ and His kingdom. Thomas Carlyle in *Heroes and Hero Worship* gave the Western world a more positive perspective by describing Muhammad as a hero with good qualities, a pious and sincere individual.

The writings of Peter the Venerable and Thomas Aquinas have provided basic perceptions of Christianity toward Muhammad and his established religion held by portions of Christians:

- Islam is a false and deliberate perversion of truth
- Islam advances by violence and the sword
- Islam promotes self-indulgence
- Muhammad is the Antichrist

About the time of Thomas Aquinas, Francis of Assisi said that Christians should disciple Muslims with love rather than with the crusading spirit. He went to Egypt in 1219 to preach to the Muslim sultan. After hearing the Muslim call to prayer, he asked for the church bells to be rung to announce worship services. He acted out of love with deliberate intentions to proclaim the Christian message to Muslims.

In Conclusion

Ram Swarup has written of the importance of the life of Muhammad to his followers, especially from their reliance upon the hadith.

> The Prophet is caught as it were in the ordinary acts of his life—sleeping, eating, mating, praying, hating, dispensing justice, planning expeditions and revenge against his enemies. The picture that emerges is hardly flattering, and one is left wondering why in the first instance it was reported at all and whether it was done by his admirers or enemies. One is also left to wonder how the believers, generation after generation, could have found this story so inspiring.
>
> The answer is that the believers are conditioned to look at the whole thing through the eyes of faith. An infidel in his fundamental misguidance may find the Prophet rather sensual and cruel—and certainly many of the things he did do not conform to ordinary ideas of morality—but the believers look at the

whole thing differently. To them morality derives from the Prophet's actions, the moral is whatever he did. Morality does not determine the Prophet's actions, but his actions determine and define morality. Muhammad's acts were not ordinary acts; they were Allah's own acts.

It was in this way and by this logic that Muhammad's opinions became the dogmas of Islam and his personal habits and idiosyncrasies became moral imperatives: Allah's commands for all believers in all ages and climes to follow.[4]

What, then, was the life of Muhammad like? In summary, Muhammad:

- Was born an orphan tribal child in Mecca in 570
- Married the wealthy widow Khadija, who provided him economic security, became one of his first converts to Islam, and gave him a daughter, Fatima
- Experienced in a cave visions from Allah through the angel Gabriel, visions which Muhammad identified as revelations and later codified into the Quran, a perfect book from God
- Preached monotheism and attacked the polytheism and animism of tribal worship at the kaba in the center of Mecca, resulting in notoriety and persecution
- Won as a convert Ali, who later married Muhammad's daughter Fatima, fathering two sons, Hasan and Husain, and becoming the first imam of the Shiites
- Escaped to Medina in 622, an event known as the Hegira; the Hegira begins the Islamic calendar
- Established the umma, the community of Islam, in Medina; built the first mosque, organized an army, and played the roles of prophet, ruler, judge, commander in chief, and prayer leader
- Subdued the tribes, including Jewish tribes, killing thousands, collecting booty including concubines, and gaining power throughout the peninsula
- Gained many wives and concubines, his favorite being Aisha, with whom he consummated marriage when she was nine years old
- Gained control of Mecca in 630, cleansed the kaba of idols, and established it as the place of pilgrimage to worship Allah
- Died and was buried in Medina in 632 with no official successor

CHAPTER 3

BELIEVE CORRECTLY, FOR THE QURAN SAYS SO

SIX BELIEFS SET IN STONE

There may not be another religion like Islam with its simplicity and unity of beliefs. Whether one is a Muslim in Singapore or Saudi Arabia, a Sunni or Shiite, a scholar or poor person, the major beliefs are the same. There is little if any argument about their broad meanings. The Quran states that it is righteousness to believe in Allah, the last day, angels, the Book, and the messengers. (Quran 2:177)

The major beliefs of Islam are the following:

- Monotheism: There is no other god than the one god Allah.
- Angels: Among the angels, Gabriel appeared to Muhammad from heaven with the words of the Quran.
- Prophets: There are many prophets, including Jesus, but Muhammad is the last prophet.
- Scriptures: The Quran is the infallible, inerrant scripture revealed to Muhammad. The Torah and the Gospel were revealed to Moses and Jesus as inerrant in their times but have since become corrupt.
- Judgment: Everyone will be judged by Allah.
- Paradise and hell: Distinctly different eternal destinies await the blessed and the damned.

Orthodox Islam accepts these beliefs with little wiggle room. Popular or folk Islam holds broadly to these beliefs but allows accretions to them. But no Muslim would deny what the Quran tells them to believe, namely, the substance of the above beliefs.

ALLAH: THE ONLY GOD

Arabic tribes worshiped many deities before Islam. There were stone and astral deities. Arab Bedouins venerated the moon, for it gave light for the nightly grazing of the herds. Islam adopted the moon as a key symbol. A crescent sits atop mosques. A lunar calendar regulates religious practices. The fasting season, Ramadan, is regulated by the rising of the moon.

There were four prominent Arabian deities. Hubal was the chief god of the kaba. There were three sister goddesses of Mecca. They were al Lat, al-Manat, and al Uzza. Muhammad at one point said that the three goddesses were deities. Later he changed his mind and said that his thinking had been corrupted by Satan. The verses of the Quran that record this are known as the "satanic verses" (see Quran 53:19–23; 22:51–53).

An ancient deity in southern Arabia known as al-Rahman became important to Muhammad. He used the name al-Rahman, which means "merciful," 169 times in the Quran to refer to the nature of Allah. With the exception of Allah, it appears more than any other descriptive term for Allah.

Among the tribes there was the idea of a supreme god, *al illah*, "the god." Poets called him "Allah." Muhammad grew up surrounded by polytheism and animism. After his visions at Mt. Hira, he began to preach the one true god, Allah. "Say that Allah is One, the Eternal God. He begot none, nor was He begotten. None is equal to Him." (Quran 112:1–4)

Allah literally means "the god." God is one and transcendent. The oneness of God precludes any plural nature of God. The transcendence of God indicates separateness from the creation.

Thus the great sin according to Islam is to associate the nature of God with creation or with humanity. The central concept of Islam is the unity of God (*tawhid*) and the quintessential sin is to associate partners or companions with the nature of God (*shirk*). God is transcendent, distant from creation and humanity. He reveals his will to humankind but not his nature.

The Quran states that Allah will not forgive idolatry. "Allah forgiveth not that partners should be set up with Him; but He forgiveth anything else, to whom He pleaseth; to set up partners with Allah is to devise a sin most heinous indeed." (Quran 4:48)

Islam rejects the Christian doctrine of the Trinity and the divinity of Jesus. The Quran accuses Christians of *shirk* in that Christians believe that Jesus is eternal and that God is triune. Islam teaches that one may have knowledge of God's law, but no one has personal or experiential knowledge of God. God reveals his law, but he does not reveal Himself.

Muslims believe that God created the universe and administers its affairs through his servants or obedient ones. The basic relationship between God and humankind is God as lord (*al Rabb*) and humankind as slaves (*Abd*). There is to be total submission to the laws of God.

The Quran requires that God be called by his beautiful names,[1] though it does not list them. (Quran 59:22–24) A tradition relates that Muhammad said there are ninety-nine names of God and to memorize and repeat them gains entry into paradise.) Scholars have grouped the names variously associated with life, knowledge, power, will, hearing, seeing, and speech. Each chapter of the Quran begins, "In the name of Allah, Most Gracious, Most Merciful."

Many Muslims use prayer beads (*tasbih*) and count off the names of God with each touch of a bead. The name Allah is used prominently in calligraphy. *Allah Akbar*, "God is Great," is sounded at worship time. Regardless of the native tongue of a Muslim, the Arabic word *Allah* is spoken countless times each day. To Muslims it is a holy name given by the angel Gabriel to the prophet Muhammad.

What Muslims believe about God is summarized in the first chapter of the Quran. It is called *Fatiha,* or "opening." It is the central prayer of Muslims and is used during the five daily prayers and on special occasions. The *Fatiha* is:

"In the name of Allah, Most Gracious, Most Merciful. Praise be to Allah the Cherisher and Sustainer of the Worlds; Most Gracious, Most Merciful. Master of the Day of Judgment. Thee do we worship, and Thine aid we seek. Show us the straight way. The way of those on whom Thou hast bestowed Thy Grace, those whose portion is not wrath and who go not astray." (1:1–7)

THE ANGEL GABRIEL BRINGS THE QURAN

Muslims believe in angels. (Quran 2:285; 6:100; 34:40–41; 46:29–32; 72:1–28) They are invisible beings who carry out the commands of God. The archangel Gabriel is the most famous. It was Gabriel who appeared to Muhammad and brought the Quran to him from heaven and told him to recite. Muslims also believe Gabriel appeared to Moses and to the virgin Mary.

Other angels include Michael, the angel of providence and guardian of the Jews; Israfil, the summoner to resurrection; and Izrail, the angel of death. (Angels protect: "We are your protectors in this life and in the hereafter." (Quran 41:31; 82:10–12) Islamic tradition teaches that two angels are assigned to each individual at birth. One records good deeds, and the other bad deeds. They go with one throughout life and remain with him until judgment day.)

God has created other spiritual beings called "jinn." They are invisible, intelligent beings with freedom of choice for good or evil, and they affect people. Some Islamic scholars consider Satan an angel, but others consider him a jinn. Satan disobeyed God by refusing to honor Adam after his creation. He caused Adam and Eve to eat the forbidden fruit in paradise.

THE TOP SIX PROPHETS

Prophets have been sent to peoples of the world with the same message from God in heaven. (Quran 2:38, 177, 252, 285; 4:80, 164; 18:110; 33:40; 17:70) A prophet was sent to every people. (Quran 10:48; 16:36; 40:15) Tradition indicates some 124,000 prophets.

Islam affirms the message of God's prophets. "We believe in Allah, and the revelation given to us, and to Abraham, Ismail, Isaac, Jacob, and the Tribes, and that given to Moses and Jesus, and that given to all Prophets from their Lord: We make no difference between one and another of them: and we bow to Allah in Islam." (Quran 2:136)

Prophets bring the Word of God. They are the purest and most righteous of men. Prophets have shared four major virtues: truth, honesty, conveying the message of God, and intelligence. They have been free from all vices. Though human, they bring the divine message. Islam is the epitome of a prophetic religion.

The Quran mentions some twenty-five prophets by name. Four are Arabs. Three are from the New Testament: Zechariah, John the Baptist, and Jesus. The rest are from the Old Testament. Thus the Quran asserts, "To every people was sent a Messenger." (10:48)

Islam gives high titles to six prophets:

- Adam is the Chosen of God
- Noah is the Preacher of God
- Abraham is the Friend of God
- Moses is the Speaker of God
- Jesus is the Word of God
- Muhammad is the Apostle of God

Jesus is named ninety-seven times in the Quran. He is referred to as messiah, word of God, spirit of God, and speech of truth. He was born of the virgin Mary, performed miracles as a child, and appeared to die on the cross. However, Muslims believe that Jesus was no more than a messenger, as those before Him. (Quran 5:75; 4:171)

Muslims utter "praise be upon him" after the name of every prophet, including Jesus. Jesus is given more honor with titles and references than any prophet before Muhammad. However, Jesus is not considered the Son of God, nor did He die on the cross. Only the name of Jesus, alongside that of Abraham, appears in every list of prophets.

Muhammad was the last and final prophet, the "seal of the prophets." The time was ripe. The message of the prophets before him had been corrupted. The message was not new, for the Quran was given to confirm all previous revelations, to correct the corruption into which the Scriptures of Moses and Jesus had fallen, and to restore God's original and only message through the prophets. That message was the same to all prophets, including the Torah of Moses and the Gospel of Jesus.

The Quran speaks of Muhammad, "O Prophet, Truly, We have sent thee as a Witness, a Bearer of Glad Tidings, and a Warner, and as one who invites to Allah's grace by His leave." (33:45–46) He was the "seal of the prophets," the last and final messenger. (33:40) He superseded all previous prophets and revelations.

All prophets from Adam to Muhammad formed an unbreakable chain. Their messages have been the same as the Quran, all from the "mother book in heaven." (Quran 43:4; 13:39) However, since their messages before Muhammad have been either lost or corrupted, Muhammad brings the final and perfect message in the Quran. He is the last prophet.

THE PERFECT QURAN:
THE PAST PERFECT TORAH AND GOSPEL

Many prophets have brought messages from God to various peoples which were inscribed into sacred books. Four books well known to Muslims are the Torah revealed to Moses, the Psalms to David, the Gospel (*Injil*) to Jesus, and the Quran to Muhammad. Jews and Christians are considered "People of the Book" because of the original revelations to Moses and Jesus.

However, Muslims believe the Torah and the Gospel have been changed and corrupted over time. Consequently, the Quran was needed to correct the errors in the corrupted books. It finalizes the truth from

God as transmitted from the archangel Gabriel, recited by the prophet Muhammad, and written down into the Arabic language.

Traditional Islam considers the Quran as identical with the "mother of the book" in heaven. The Quran contains the very words of God. (Quran 85:21–22; 43:3–4; 13:39) God's revelation came not through a person but through a written record. Islam then is a book religion. It was revealed from Gabriel to Muhammad in the Arabic language. Arabic thus becomes intertwined with the revelation itself. Any translation into another language loses its original authenticity.

Traditional Islam views the Quran as a miracle. Therefore literary or historical criticism of the Quran is unacceptable. To question or defame the Quran is to do the same to God. Orthodox Islam has generally affirmed that the Quran is uncreated. It is God's word and a quality of God's nature. Some scholars teach that Muhammad's speech in delivering the Quran verbally iterates divine speech.

The Quran is composed of 114 chapters or *suras*, and each chapter has verses or *ayas*. There are 6,616 verses and 77,934 words. Muslims are challenged to memorize all of it and to recite it in the mosques and in daily prayers. Eighty-six chapters were revealed in Mecca, and twenty-eight in Medina.

The chapters in the Quran are not in chronological order. It is often suggested that it reads better chronologically from back to front. The Meccan chapters deal with patience and perseverance and idolatry, indicating the problems and challenges Muhammad faced at Mecca. The Medina chapters have information on politics, legislation, and the settlement of disputes which indicate the establishment of the early community in Medina.

From the night the angel Gabriel came to Muhammad and told him to recite until his death (610–632), the Prophet received revelations from God. After Muhammad's death Caliph Abu Bakr collected the revelations into one document from the memorizations of the Prophet's companions. Under Caliph Uthman in 652, the Quran was canonized. It has served as the authorized version.

Inspiration of the Quran has been interpreted variously by Muslim scholars. There was physical and psychological stress upon Muhammad as he encountered the angel Gabriel, who gave him the words to recite. The Quran indicates that Muhammad even thought he might be possessed by a demon. Some observers have suggested hallucinations, epileptic seizures, and even demon possession.

However, over one billion Muslims believe it is the unquestioned perfect word of God. It contains guidance for all matters of life and the afterlife. Muslims memorize it, recite it, and create artistic expressions from it. Many believe they receive double rewards by memorizing and reciting it which gains them a place in heaven.

Seyyed Hossein Nasr, an Islamic scholar, wrote, "The soul of a Muslim is like a mosaic made up of formulae of the Quran in which he breathes and lives."* A Muslim who memorizes the Quran is called a *Hafiz*. A tradition reports that the prophet Muhammad said, "Such a person as recites the Quran and masters it by heart will be with the noble righteous scribes in heaven. And such a person as exerts himself to learn the Quran by heart and recites it with great difficulty will have a double reward."[3]

THE DAY OF JUDGMENT AND RESURRECTION

Islam emphasizes judgment, rewards, and destiny. As God created all, so God judges all. One lives life either to attain bliss in heaven or damnation in hell. (Quran 55; 4:45; 14:16–17) Thus there is an end to the world, a day of resurrection and a time of judgment, and the distribution of rewards.

For Islam resurrection and judgment day are virtually the same belief and event. The Quran refers to the coming day of judgment more than any other topic except monotheism. Muhammad preached of the future judgment when truth would be revealed. He explained the judgment in language the merchants of his day could understand. Accounts would be settled and scales would be balanced.

The judgment day is described in various ways: day of wrath, day of decision, day of retribution, and day of truth. Not only individuals with their guardian angels but nations will assemble before the great Judge Allah, and their deeds will be weighed.

Traditions (hadith) describe precursors of judgment day. Religious knowledge will decrease. Ignorance will prevail. Open and illegal sexual intercourse will increase. The number of women will increase over men so that fifty women will be cared for by one man.

The final hour will come suddenly, and great despair will overtake unbelievers. There are scenes of apocalyptic doom. Natural disasters will occur. Graves will be opened. (Quran chapters 82; 84; chapter 75 is entitled "The Resurrection.")

Each individual will stand before God. "On the Day of Judgment We shall bring out for him a scroll, which he will see spread open. It will be said to him, Read thine own record. Sufficient is thy soul this day to make out an account against thee." (Quran 17:13–14)

People will call upon Muhammad to intercede before God on their behalf, but the prophet's intercession will not change any decrees of

Fifty Muslim Terms You Need to Know

Ali   Son-in-law of the Prophet Muhammad; married the prophet's daughter Fatima; first imam of the Iranian Shiites; fourth caliph in the Sunni tradition.

Allah   Arabic name for God; means "the God." (Allahu Akbar means Greater is God.)

Aya   A verse of the Quran; a chapter is *sura.*

Ayatollah   A religious leader among the Shiites who is given high authority.

Bismalah   The general Islamic invocation to God: "In the name of the merciful Lord of mercy," which prefaces every chapter (sura) of the Quran except sura 9.

Dar al-Harb   "House of War"; the areas of the world that are still ignorant and disobedient and unsubdued by Islam.

Dar al-Islam   "House of Islam"; the geographical realm of the world in which Islam is in full devotional, political, and legal actuality. In Islamic constitutional law, the world is divided into Dar al-Harb (territory not under the rule of Islam) and Dar al-Islam (territory under the rule of Islam); Dar al-Harb should be brought under Islam either by surrender or warfare.

Dawah   "Call"; missionary; organization for the missionary activity of Islam.

Doa   Nonritual prayer as distinct from *salat,* which is formal prayer.

Fatima   Daughter of the prophet Muhammad; wife of Ali the first Imam.

Gabriel   The angel through whom Allah revealed the Quran to Muhammad.

Hadith   "Tradition"; reports of the words, actions, and attitudes of the prophet Muhammad, constituting a body of literature second only to the Quran in authority for Muslims.

Haj   Pilgrimage to Mecca and its environs; one of the pillars (required practices in the Quran) for Muslims.

Hijra   Hegira; the flight or emigration of Muhammad and his followers from Mecca to Medina in 622; the Islamic lunar calendar begins with this date as A.H. 1 (After the Hegira).

Husain   Son of Ali; grandson of prophet Muhammad; third Imam of the Shiites; Iranian Shiites revere him with the narrative and drama of his death.

Id al-Fitr   The feast and celebration of ending the fasting month of Ramadan which is required of Muslims and is one of the pillars of Islam.

Id al-Adha	The feast that celebrates the conclusion of the pilgrimage to Mecca; a lamb or other animal is sacrificed by the pilgrims in Mecca as well as by Muslims worldwide.
Imam	A general term among all Muslims for leader of the congregational prayer in the mosque; also among Sunni Muslims, it is the Caliph; among Shiite Muslims, it is one of the descendants of Ali recognized by Allah as supreme ruler of the world.
Injil	"Gospel"; revelation or book given by Allah to Jesus (Isa); Muslims believe that since Jesus the Gospel has been corrupted in its present form in the Bible.
Islam	The faith, obedience, and practice of peoples who follow the teachings of the Quran and the tradition of prophet Muhammad; the final, perfect religion of Allah; "submission to Allah."
Jihad	The concept of extraordinary effort in the belief and practice of Islam; often understood as a militancy in defending and/or extending the interests of Islam.
Jinn	Invisible spirits referred to in the Quran.
Kaba	"Cube"; the central sanctuary in the great house of pilgrimage in Mecca made of grey stone and covered by a black curtain; pilgrims circumambulate it in the pilgrimage rituals; Muslims are required all over the world to face Mecca and the kaba for their daily prayers.
Kafir	Infidel; unbeliever.
Khadija	A wealthy widow who became the first wife of prophet Muhammad; great encourager and first follower in establishment of Islam.
Khums	"1/5"; a religious tax; 1/5 of actual income paid to religious authorities.
Madrasa	A school designated for Islamic studies; generally associated with a mosque.
Mahdi	"The divinely guided One"; often associated with the Twelfth and Hidden Imam of the Iranian Shiites.
Masjid	"Place of prostration"; a mosque, the building in which Muslims pray and gather for religious and social occasions; its major features are the minaret, the mihrab, and the mimbar.
Mecca	The holy city of Islam; birthplace of prophet Muhammad; Muslims face Mecca in daily prayers; the city of the required pilgrimage.
Medina	The second holy city of Islam; Muhammad fled to the city in 622; the city in which the Muslim religion and community (umma) was established; place of tomb of Muhammad.

Muhammad	Prophet of Islam (570–632); born in Mecca; buried in Medina.
Mujahidun	Soldiers of Allah.
Muslim	One who believes in, belongs to, and performs Islam; "one who submits."
Quran	The holy book of Islam; the revelation of Allah through angel Gabriel to prophet Muhammad; 114 chapters (suras); "recitation."
Ramadan	The ninth month of the Muslim calendar; the month of obligatory fasting as required in the Quran; the 27th of Ramadan concludes the fast.
Rasul	Messenger; apostle; title of Muhammad.
Salam	Peace; the greeting Muslims exchange with one another.
Salat	Ritual prayer performed five times daily; one of the required pillars of Islam in the Quran; different from *doa* prayer, which is voluntary and informal. *Salat al Fajr* (dawn prayer); *Salat al Zuhr* (midday prayer); *Salat al Asr* (afternoon prayer); *Salat al Maghrib* (evening prayer after sunset); *Salat al Isha* (late evening prayer).
Shahada	Witness or confession; the first required pillar of Islam; "there is no god but God, and Muhammad is the messenger of God."
Sharia	Sacred and canon law based on the Quran (God's revelation), *Hadith* (sayings and traditions of prophet Muhammad), *Ijma* (consensus decision by the Muslim authorities), and *Qiyas* (reasoning by analogy); the path of duty both ritual and general behavior for Muslims.
Shiite	"Partisan"; follower of the branch of Islam that accepts Ali as the legitimate successor to Muhammad; believe the descendants of Muhammad should rule the Islamic community; Iran is the primary Shiite Muslim state.
Shirk	"Association"; the act (sin) of regarding anything as equal with Allah; idolatry, polytheism, or attributing divinity to anyone; Muslims view Christianity as idolatrous for equating Jesus (as Son of God and member of the Trinity) with God.
Sufi	A Muslim mystic; Sufism is Islamic mysticism. It seeks direct experience with God; it has leaders called Sheikhs and communities called brotherhoods.
Sunna	The path of tradition or orthodoxy followed by Muslims.
Sunni	Term which means those who follow tradition of reliance on the Quran and the Hadith and are called Sunnis; approved leader to follow prophet Muhammad by consensus rather than the Shiite idea of family successorship.

Sura	A chapter of the Quran; the Quran has 114 *suras*.
Ulama	Scholars of Islamic theology or law; singular is Alim.
Umma	The community of Islam; the solidarity of faith and prayer; the political incorporation of the Islamic religion.
Zakat	Almsgiving; a required pillar of Islam in the Quran.

damnation. The resurrection of the body will occur. (Muslims bury the dead, prohibiting cremation.)

After the earth has perished, people will be revived or resurrected with the blast of a trumpet. Deeds will be weighed and assessed with the opening of the Book of Deeds. God will dispense absolute justice.

A Sunni tradition tells of the return of Jesus as messiah. He breaks the cross, kills pigs, dies, and is buried beside Muhammad. Another tradition teaches that a messiah will come and destroy the Antichrist. The eschatological figure in Islam is known as the *Mahdi,* the one to return and bring the world to judgment and Satan to submission.

In the final judgment scene, God calculates the direction of the tipping of the scales. If they tip to righteousness, the person being judged will dwell in the garden or paradise. If they tip to evil, the person's destiny will be the fire or hell. It is a solemn moment. There appears to be no last-minute or deathbed conversions in Islam. (Quran 4:18)

EITHER THE GARDEN (HEAVEN) OR FIRE (HELL)

This prayer is attributed to an eighth-century Muslim woman:

O God, if I worship Thee in fear of Hell, Burn me in Hell. If I worship Thee in hope of Paradise, exclude me from Paradise. But If I worship Thee for Thine Own Sake, Withhold not from me Thine eternal beauty.

Islam teaches its followers to worship God and requires them to obey God. The Quran forcefully commands the people to believe the God who judges and promises the rewards of heaven and hell as well as to obey the God who requires prayer, fasting, and pilgrimage, the acts of obedience that lead to righteousness. Righteousness leads to the garden of paradise.

Muslims who follow the straight path of Islam may look forward to heaven or paradise. It is a garden of refreshment and beauty. There are full streams of clean water. There are rivers of milk and fountains of honey. There is a permanent oasis with trees of luscious fruits.

Satan is banished from paradise. The presence of Allah is enjoyed. Paradise offers both sensual and sexual delights. For men there are

29

beautiful virgins (*houris*). (Quran 3:14–15; 47:15; 55: section 3) There are various quarters in heaven to which one may aspire. In some traditions, wives are kept in separate quarters where their husbands may discreetly visit them. Married men are described as having new wives who are sensual, charming, and eternally youthful.

Another tradition teaches that only Muslims will be admitted to paradise. Jews and Christians are excluded, though considered "People of the Book." Soldiers and martyrs are given a special place. In Muhammad's time, martyrdom might result from following his command, spreading Islam by fighting the enemy, and losing one's life in battle. A martyr gained immediate entry into heaven with priority status. Heaven was so good that the martyr would be willing to die again.

The Quran describes hell as a roasting place, as pus, as boiling water. Vivid torture is depicted with boiling brains and molten lead poured into ears. It is a burning and odious place. It is the abode of idolaters, unbelievers, and the unrepentant. They will wear clothing of liquid pitch with their faces covered with fire. (Quran 14:50; 76:4)

One tradition reports Muhammad as saying that he stood at the gate of the fire and saw that women were the majority entering hell. Another tradition tells of the prophet's describing a woman who is assigned the hellfire for tying a cat and refusing it food or freedom. Women are singled out as perhaps more deserving of hell than men.

Islamic beliefs do not include the concept of original sin. One is responsible for one's own sins and disobedience. No one can take away sin or die for the sin of another. One must submit to God for forgiveness and justice. There is no depravity in human nature; there is ignorance and weakness. Salvation is a future state after the judgment when one is delivered from hell and gains heaven.

Islam teaches predestination (*qadar*). God foreknows and decrees all happenings according to his will and wisdom. Yet humans are free and responsible. They have freedom of action but not freedom of results, for the laws of God control actions and results. Muslims must have correct knowledge and ritual so that their consequences will cause good and not evil.

And the Quran Goes On

The Quran is the final authority and arbiter on all Muslim beliefs. It states, "Yea, to Allah belongs all that is in the heavens and on earth: so that He rewards those who do evil, according to their deeds, and He rewards those who do good, with what is best." (53:31)

CHAPTER 4

LIVING THE GOOD LIFE

How to Get to Heaven

THE STRAIGHT PATH

A favorite expression among Muslims is *Enshallah,* "if Allah wills." Much of Islam is predicated upon predestination, even though Muslims believe they must do all within their power to please God in order to obtain rewards in heaven. The Quran marks out the straight path (1:6; 6:154), and of all world religions Islam has the clearest and most concise description of how to please God.

The Quran requires Muslims to follow five basic practices, sometimes called the five pillars of Islam. These include the great confession, prayers, almsgiving, the fast of Ramadan, and the pilgrimage to Mecca. Another practice is jihad, the struggle to extend Islam to the non-Muslim world.

These practices are uniform and regular, across cultures and languages. They follow set times of the day, month, and year. The stated prayers must be repeated in the Arabic language. Individuals can practice these in isolation, though most are shared in community. The mosque, which means a place of prayer, is where Muslims gather for prayer and worship. Outside the home it is the center for religious activities.

Muslims believe in their heads there is one God; there are angels, prophets, sacred scriptures, and the great judgment day for heaven or hell. They believe in their hearts that to keep the pillars of Islam is to

31

get them nearer to heaven. The pillars are demanding. They are time-consuming. The Quran requires them. One does not question them.

THE GREAT CREED OF ISLAM

Seven Arabic words repeated by every Muslim describe the very core of Islam. *"Ilaha illa Allah. Muhammad rasul Allah."* "There is no god but God. Muhammad is the messenger of God." This is the *shahada*, the great confession. (Quran 3:81; 5:83–84; 2:255; 3:18; 3:144; 4:87; 7:172; 33:40; 48:29; 64:8) It is said that to say these words and believe them is conversion to Islam and is what makes a Muslim a Muslim.

The shahada subsumes Islam's major beliefs:

- Belief in one God alone; there is no other.
- Belief in angels; they do the will of God.
- Belief in sacred books, including the Torah, the Gospel (Injil), and the Quran.
- Belief in prophets, including Abraham, Moses, Jesus, and Muhammad.
- Belief in the resurrection, judgment day, heaven, and hell.

These words of the shahada are whispered into a Muslim's ears at birth and at death. This confession is uttered fourteen times daily in the stated prayers. Muslims confess their monotheistic faith and their final prophet.

There are no other gods. Allah is God. God is creator, sustainer, and lord. Muslims are accountable only to him. There were other prophets. But Muhammad is the last and final prophet.

Muslims honor and follow the life of Muhammad, both his public and private life. Thus, the confession provides the road map for life. Belief and practice fit together in submission to God and acknowledgment of the example of the final prophet. It unites the vertical and the horizontal, the spiritual and the ethical. God is the focus of worship and prayer. Muhammad is the role model for the individual and the community.

PRAYERS: LIFELINE OF MUSLIMS

Muslims are known for their prayers (*salah*). Prayers are vocal and visible, orderly and timely, intentional and directional. There are five stated times of prayer daily. They may be done individually or in community, at home, at work, or in the mosque. But the Quran requires that they must be accomplished. (Quran 2:3, 177; 11:114; 17:78; 20:14, 130; 30:17–18)

The central prayer of Muslims is the Fatiha. Used on all special occasions and during the five daily prayers, it has been characterized as serving the same purpose for Muslims that the Lord's Prayer does for Christians: "In the name of Allah, Most Gracious, Most Merciful. Praise be to Allah the Cherisher and Sustainer of the Worlds. Most Gracious, Most Merciful; Master of the Day of Judgment. Thee do we worship, and Thine aid we seek. Show us the straight path." (Quran 1:1–6)

The times of prayer are regulated daily. The *subh* prayer may be given from dawn to sunrise. *Zuhr* prayer occurs between noon and mid-afternoon. *Asr* prayer may be from mid-afternoon to sunset. *Maghrib* prayer is from sunset to the disappearance of the evening twilight. *Isha* prayer may be from the twilight to the coming of dawn.

A prayer leader ascends the steps of the minaret in the mosque and calls the people to prayer at the stated times. He chants in Arabic, "God is great. There is no god but God, and Muhammad is the messenger of God. Come to prayer. Come to prayer. Come to success in this life and the hereafter." Many mosques now have recordings and amplification systems for the call to prayer.

✳The mosque has a source of water for ablution. Before prayer, each Muslim washes the hands, rinses the mouth, cleans the nose, washes the face and forearms, and washes the feet up to the ankles. Cleansing, prayer, and forgiveness are intertwined.

A Muslim stands and kneels during prayer. These actions are called *rakahs*. Parts of the Quran are recited in Arabic. Although prayers may be uttered anywhere except at cemeteries or rest rooms, they are especially efficacious when said with others in the mosque. The mosque (*masjid*) means a place of prostration. A prayer leader (imam) stands before neat rows of Muslims, faces Mecca, and leads them in words and *rakahs*. A niche (*mihrab*) in the mosque's wall points the direction to Mecca. The sermon is given from a raised platform (*mimbar*). Friday is the "day of congregation." Muslims go to the mosque on Fridays to say their noon prayers and to hear the weekly sermon.

Islam has no ordained clergy. Leaders are often selected according to their knowledge of Islam and the beauty of their voices in oratory, in the call to prayer, and in reciting the Quran in Arabic.

Besides the five stated formal prayers, there are informal prayers (*doas*). These are extemporaneous petitions, pleas, and praises to God and to Islamic heroes. They may be voiced in one's native language. *Doas* are often associated with tombs and mosques dedicated to Muslim saints and heroes. These prayers express the more emotional and heartfelt side of folk Islam.

The Islamic calendar provides many special times for prayers such as Muhammad's birthday and Ramadan (the month of fasting). Haj, the pilgrimage season, requires prayers at specific times and places in and around Mecca. Thus much of a Muslim's life is regulated by prayer and spent in prayer.

Author talks with Muslim leader in courtyard of the central mosque in downtown Nairobi.

ALMSGIVING: POSSESSIONS AND PERCENTAGES

Giving of possessions for the cause of Islam, known as *zakat*, is required in the Quran. (2:43, 83, 110, 177, 277; 9:60, 103; 24:56; 27:3; 57:7; 59:7; 98:5) Muslims are reminded that what they own belongs to God and that they are God's trustees of their wealth and goods. *Zakat* is two and a half percent of one's wealth. The root word of *zakat* means "to be pure." Giving signifies the purifying of one's soul.

In some Muslim nations *zakat* is a required tax, and *zakat* stamps may be purchased from post offices. However, much giving is voluntary, and mosques and the poor are supported by gifts. A Muslim endowment (*waqf*) is money or property designated to build mosques, libraries, hospitals, and schools. In many places, worshipers place money in a metal box at the door of the mosque.

Good deeds such as loaning a camel or giving a smile to a neighbor are considered gifts called *sadaqat*. These are different from the legal alms of *zakat*. Muhammad affirmed the dignity of work in contrast to begging. He counseled, however, to give help to the needy. A tradition reports that Muhammad told the story of two angels who come down from heaven every day. One angel says that God will compensate every person who contributes to God's cause. The other angel says that God will destroy every miser.

RAMADAN: THE FASTING SEASON

Ramadan is the ninth month of the Islamic lunar calendar. During this month, Gabriel revealed the Quran to Muhammad. Serious Muslims fast during Ramadan, for the Quran prescribes it for all believers. (2:183–185)

Fasting must be observed during daylight hours in Ramadan. There is to be no drinking, eating, frivolity, or sexual intercourse. Traditions relate that fasting is a screen from hell. Thus one draws closer to paradise by submitting to the law of God. The fast is broken daily by eating after sunset and before dawn.

One is encouraged to listen to or to read the Quran during the month. The Quran is divided into thirty equal portions to make it easier to read.

Exemptions from the requirement include aged adults, pregnant women, children, and youth before puberty. Rather than fast, a Muslim may make it up later or give food to the poor.

The fasting season concludes at the end of Ramadan. The festival of Id Fitr (breaking the fast) is celebrated with visitations, meetings, and meals. During this time, many buy new clothes, attend special meetings at the mosque, and prepare to return to normal routines.

Because the Muslim calendar is based on the lunar year, Ramadan falls sometimes in winter and sometimes in summer. Because the fast includes abstaining from water, fasting is especially difficult in the hot summer. Some orthodox will not even swallow their saliva. Ramadan is the season to test one's endurance and self-denial. Many say fasting is good for the health. It is a time to give food, which one would otherwise consume, to the poor. Thus, one observes one's moral duties and feels drawn closer to heaven.

GOING TO MECCA ON PILGRIMAGE

Mecca is the holiest city of Islam. It is the birthplace of Muhammad. It is the city faced by over a billion Muslims each time they pray. It is the city of the required pilgrimage. Only Muslims may enter it.

Tradition associates the prophet Abraham with Mecca. Abraham had a son, Ishmael, by his concubine, Hagar. Hagar and Ishmael were stranded in a desert place. In need of water, she discovered a nearby well, which came to be known as Zamzam. Around the well the town of Mecca sprang up.

✳ Also, Abraham had a dream to offer his son, Ishmael, as a sacrifice to God. Instead, a ram was offered, and Abraham built a place of worship in commemoration. It was called the kaba, and people were invited to make an annual pilgrimage to it. The pilgrimage became known as the haj.

Arabs corrupted the religion of Abraham with their polytheistic practices to some 360 idols at the kaba. Muhammad removed the idols from the kaba and made it the focus of Islam with the worship of Allah, the direction of prayer, and the annual pilgrimage. The kaba contains a black stone that ancient tradition holds was a fallen meteorite.

The present day kaba is forty feet long, thirty-three feet wide, and fifty feet high. A black cloth engraved in gold threads with Quranic sayings covers it. The black stone, about 12 inches in diameter, is placed in the eastern corner of the kaba.[1]

Several million Muslims go on pilgrimage to Mecca each year. It is called the Greater Haj and is mandatory in the Quran. The Quran requires every man and woman who is physically and financially able to make at least one haj in a lifetime. (2:196–201; 3:97; 22:26–29) In preparation the pilgrims dress in unsewn white material to demonstrate their unity and egalitarianism. They cannot cut their hair or nails, use cosmetics, or have sexual relations. This state of purity and consecration is called Ihram. Pilgrims are now prepared to enter Mecca to formally begin the haj.

During one day the pilgrims circumambulate, or walk around, the kaba seven times reciting prayers and the Quran. They then run seven times between two hills in Mecca, recalling Hagar's frantic search for water for her son Ishmael. The pilgrims at last take a drink from the well of Zamzam that had sprung up to satisfy Hagar and Ishmael's needs.

Then they travel thirteen miles to the plain of Arafat near the Mount of Mercy, where Muhammad gave his last sermon. They stand from noon to sunset in reverence and prayer to commemorate

Muhammad's standing in the community. Muhammad taught that the best of prayers is the prayer on the day of Arafat.

On another day, pilgrims go to Mina, the place where Abraham is said to have sacrificed Ishmael. Three stone pillars represent places where Satan tempted Ishmael to rebel against his father's attempt to obey God. Ishmael stood against Satan by throwing stones at him. The pilgrims reenact Ishmael's resistance toward Satan by throwing seven stones at each stone pillar while saying *"Allah Akbaer,"* "God is Great." Thus they are resisting temptation.

After resisting temptation, they offer an animal sacrifice. It is called *Id Adhan,* the feast of the sacrifice. The sacrifice is a reminder of the ram Abraham sacrificed in place of his son Ishmael. Much of the food is given away to the poor and needy. Muslims around the world are also simultaneously observing the feast in identification with the pilgrims on haj. In this way they vicariously experience haj with them.

Another day they return to Mecca. They circumambulate the kaba seven times and run between the hills another seven times. Thus they conclude the rites of the pilgrimage, cutting their hair and changing to their regular clothing. They assume the title of "haji," those who have completed the required haj of Allah as commanded in the Quran.

Some visit the city of Medina 250 miles north of Mecca. There are the mosque of the prophet Muhammad and his grave. It is particularly important to pray at the mosque. The graves of Abu Bakr, Umar, and Fatima are also in Medina.

The pilgrimage to Mecca is the highlight of a Muslim's life. Upon returning home there are gifts shared, large gatherings with meals and story telling, and a new status in the community for the pilgrim now known as a haji.

Besides the required Greater Haj, there is the Lesser Haj. Muslims may go to Mecca any time of the year to perform a shorter haj. They change to pilgrim clothing, circle the kaba, and run between the hills in Mecca. However, it is not a substitute for the required haj.

Muhammad said that the kaba was an inviolable place; it was *haram.* God had made it a sanctuary since the creation of the heavens and the earth and would remain so until the day of resurrection.

SPREADING ISLAM BY FAITH AND FIGHTING: JIHAD

Islamic teachings divide the world into two spheres. There is the way of heedlessness or ignorance, known as *al Jahiliyya.* And there is the way of submission to God, known as *al Islam.* Humans have two choices. Either they are ignorant and disobedient to God and live in the territory of nonsubmission or war, known as *dar al harb.* Or they are obedient and submissive to God and live in the territory of Islam, known as *dar al Islam*.

The mission of Islam is to deal with the sphere of disobedience and ignorance and war and bring the peoples of this sphere under Islam through conversion or influence or submission. Jihad is the way to accomplish this mission. (Quran 2:244; 9:5; 9:29; 22:78; 47:4; 49:15)

There are two understandings of jihad. The basic meaning is "to struggle" or "to strive." Greater jihad is the warfare against sin and all that is against God and the teachings of the Quran. It is the personal struggle each Muslim wages to be a true believer and follower. The Quran urges one to stay on the straight path and to strive in Allah's cause. (22:78; 49:15)

Lesser jihad is the traditional holy war launched in the name of God against the enemies of God and Islam. Thus, jihad is both a personal and community commitment to defend and spread the religion of Islam.

Muslims popularly refer to four expressions of jihad:

- Jihad of the Tongue: speaking about their faith
- Jihad of the Hand: expressing their faith in good works
- Jihad of the Heart: making their faith a force for good
- Jihad of the Sword: defending their faith when under attack

Both non-Muslim and Muslim writers have used the phrase "holy war" with reference to jihad. Muslim scholars, however, write that Islam teaches it is unholy to start war although some wars are inevitable and justifiable.[2]

The Quran urges those to fight for the cause of Allah and kill pagans wherever they are found. Whenever believers meet unbelievers, Muslims are encouraged to smite their neck and to fight those who believe not in Allah and the last day. (2:244; 47:4; 9:5; 9:29)

Tradition approves of violence against infidels and those who leave Islam as their native or chosen religion. Fighting and killing are described as beloved activities. Apostasy is punishable by death.

In the traditions, Muhammad is asked which deed is the dearest to Allah. He responded: to offer prayers at their fixed times, to be good and dutiful to one's parents, and to participate in jihad (religious fighting) in Allah's cause, in that order.

The Quran and the traditions present jihad as coercive and violent. Muslims understand it to be an effort or struggle to bring righteousness and peace on the earth. However, the history of jihad also has revealed it to be warfare against tribes, peoples, and nations whom Islam considers to be its enemies.

There are different rewards for the practice of jihad. They include rewards for punishing non-Muslims and for being a martyr (*Shahid*). Martyrdom guarantees a place in paradise and an honorable name bestowed upon one's family. (Quran 47:4–5)

A Muslim writer in the United States stated that the hardest struggle (jihad) is to "implement the rule of God on earth." Yet it is the duty of every Muslim to convince the majority that Islam is a God-given system of life that is far superior to any man-made system.

> Muslims have a duty to establish an environment of freedom of expression to enable them to convey the message of Islam. If there is a tyrannical government which does not allow the freedom of presenting Islam to the people, the Muslims have a duty to obtain a free environment by the best possible means of the time . . . It is the hardest of the struggles (jihad), that is, to implement the rule of God on earth. In a given geographical territory a system already exists; therefore it is not easy to tell the followers of that system that there are flaws in their system and you would like to offer an alternative; people do not look at such ideas sympathetically. Nevertheless, it is the duty of every Muslim to convince the majority that Islam is a God-given system of life, and it is far, far superior to any man-made system.[3]

Islam prides itself on having the perfect word of God, the last prophet, the correct beliefs, the indisputable practices, and the answers for the social, economic, political, and religious matters of life. It is Islam as the superior religion versus the non-Islamic world. Kenneth Cragg, a noted Christian scholar on Islam, has written that to study the history and theology of Islam "is to encounter the most resolute and unperturbed of all faiths in placing trust, and finding pride, in political religion."[4]

Jihad, then, becomes a method to persuade, coerce, subdue, and tolerate others until Islam is established. For some peoples like Jews and Christians who are considered "People of the Book," there is a poll tax to be paid and restrictions to their religious practices as they are tolerated in the Islamic sphere.

A MUSLIM FOR ALL SEASONS

As Regular as the Lunar Calendar

Good Muslims pray daily at sunrise, noon, and sunset. Friday is the day of noon prayers and weekly sermon when they gather as community in the mosque. During certain months special celebrations are observed, such as fasting, pilgrimage, and remembering the prophet's birthday or other pivotal times in Islam. Festivals (*ids*) are held on days to complete religious duties.

The calendar follows the lunar year rather than the solar year followed in the West. The new moon determines the first of the month. (Quran 10:6) The average interval between consecutive new moons is twenty-nine days, twelve hours, forty-four minutes, and three seconds. Lunar months alternate between twenty-nine and thirty days. A given month may have twenty-nine days in some years and thirty days in others. There are twelve months in the lunar year or 354 days on average.

The Islamic calendar travels backward through the solar calendar about eleven days each year, returning to the same solar time in about thirty-three lunar years. Thus thirty-three lunar years equal thirty-two solar years. The calendar begins on the day of the hegira, the flight from Mecca to Medina, which occurred in September 622. Therefore the Muslim calendar began with 1 A.H. (After Hegira), corresponding to A.D. 622. Our year 2000 is 1378 A.H.

Celebrations in the Lunar Year

The names of the twelve months in the Muslim calendar are:

Muharram	Safar
Rabi' I	Rabi' II
Jamadi I	Jamadi II
Rajab	Sha'ban
Ramadan	Shawwal
Dhu al Qu'da	Dhu al Hijja

Some major festivals and observances during these months are:

First of Muharram: The first day of Muharram is the New Year. It commemorates the hegira.

Tenth of Muharram: Ashura is the tenth day of Muharram when Muslims may fast. Shiite Muslims observe this day in memory of the assassination of Husain, the son of Ali and grandson of Muhammad. Passion plays and parades are rituals of the time.

Twelfth of Rabi' I: The birthday of the prophet Muhammad. Often it is an occasion for excessive veneration of Muhammad.

Twenty-seventh of Rajab: This is the night, according to tradition, when Muhammad was taken on a winged animal from Mecca to the present Dome of the Rock area. There he met the prophets who preceded him, including Jesus (Isa). He ascended to heaven and then was taken back to Mecca on the same night. There are prayers and Quranic readings on this night.

Fourteenth of Shaban: The night of repentance is a time, according to tradition, when God descends to the lowest heaven to call to man and grant forgiveness of his sins. In India and Malaysia it is a night when prayers are said for the dead, food is given to the poor, and sweets are eaten.

Ramadan: Muslims are commanded by the Quran to fast from sunrise to sunset. After sunset and prayers, Muslims may take a meal. It is inappropriate for tourists and non-Muslims to eat and drink openly in Muslim communities during Ramadan.

Twenty-seventh of Ramadan: The next to the last night of the fasting month, the time when the angel Gabriel brought the first revelation to Muhammad. Some Muslims pray during the entire night.

First of Shawwal: The day after the fasting season ends. The festival, Id Fitr, is the feast of breaking the fast. It is a happy time of family and friends visiting around meals, exchanging presents, and giving pastries and sweets.

Dhu al Hijjah 1–10: The time of the haj, the required pilgrimage to the kaba in Mecca once in a lifetime. The haj takes ten days to accomplish. Muslims worldwide come by the millions to the place where, tradition holds, prophet Abraham offered to sacrifice his son Ishmael, son of Hagar, to God.

Tenth of Dhu al Hijjah: This festival signifies the conclusion of the haj. Muslims celebrate the feast of sacrifice, Id Adhan, by offering up sheep, cows, or camels. All worldwide Muslims, whether they have made the haj to Mecca or not, perform the sacrifice. It is a festive time of much visitation, feasting, exchange of gifts, and buying of new clothes.

Mosques and Shrines

The mosque is a major institution for religious and social life. Mosque comes from the word *masjid*, "a place of prostration or prayer." (Quran 9:17–19) A Muslim may pray the stated prayers at home or work or on the way in travel. However, there is encouragement to pray with the community in the mosque.[5]

Mosques are in various sizes, shapes, and places. Invariably, they include a central prayer room with rugs or mats on the floor for sitting and kneeling during the rituals. Also present are the *mihrab*, a niche in the wall pointing the direction of prayers toward Mecca and the *mimbar*, an elevated platform (pulpit) with ascending steps from which the sermon is delivered.

Beside the mosque is a minaret, a spiraling column with a stairwell. From its top the call to prayer is sounded at the proper times. Several minarets may adorn the mosque. A pool or other source of water is inside or in the courtyard for the purification rites before prayer.

Larger mosques may include a library, social hall, rooms for Quranic study, and quarters for the resident leader. A large, central mosque may have a school for training the *ulama*, Islamic scholars. Besides providing a place for prayer, mosques serve social functions of conversation, marriage-matching of sons and daughters by parents, and sometimes places for governments to voice their programs.

Orthodox tradition permits no pictures or wall hangings in mosques. Arabic calligraphy of the Quran is dominant in mosque art. Qurans are usually available on racks. Often there is a container for money gifts.

A large mosque in a city or country may serve as a national mosque. It may have significance for worldwide Islam because of its history and prestige. It is similar to a museum or a shrine attracting pilgrims and tourists. Examples include the Dome of the Rock and the al Aqsa mosque in Jerusalem, the prophet's mosque in Damascus, and the Imam Reza Shrine mosque in Meshed, Iran. Many Muslim nations have a national mosque, often the mosque of the king or president.

A shrine is a mosque built by wealthy donors or by devotees to honor a particular Islamic figure. Most are named after members of the family of the prophet Muhammad, of his close associates, or of the imams.

A shrine may become a place of pilgrimage where Muslims visit to pray, to make vows in the name of the figure of the mosque, and to request miracles. In large shrines there are religious personnel who chant the Quran and who make prayers in mediation to saints. Most shrines are small and located in villages and places distant from urban areas and known to the local people.

A good Muslim may attend the mosque daily for prayers and weekly on Friday for the community prayers and sermon. And a good Muslim, while going to a traditional mosque for formal prayers, may also slip off to a shrine for personal prayers and assistance from a saint for miracles. While orthodox Islamic leaders may condemn shrine activities, Muslims continue to attend them.

Preachers and Priests

Islam claims no ordained clergy. Orthodoxy denies any mediatorship between a class of religious clergy and laypersons. Even so, there is a whole category of religious leaders, and theological schools train individuals for roles in mosques and Muslim communities.

Oratory is very important in the Muslim tradition. The Quran must be properly and beautifully chanted. Because it was revealed in the Arabic language, Arabic specialists are needed to interpret it. It is popularly stated that any good Muslim with a strong voice can lead the people in prayer in the mosque. Yet there are numerous specialists who lead Muslims.

The general term under which leaders are referred is *ulama*. Titles vary across Sunni and Shiite traditions as well as cultural areas. Various categories of the ulama are:

- Jurists and judges who serve the court and legal systems in interpreting and applying Islamic *sharia* law
- Preachers who ascend the *mimbar* in the mosques to deliver Friday sermons and other addresses during special seasons of the calendar
- Pastor types who attend to the needs of a mosque community through leading prayer, giving sermons, providing counsel, and administering mosque affairs and Quranic school and studies
- Specialists in folk Islam who attend the shrines in assisting pilgrims and worshipers in prayers, offerings, and vows to named saints and folk heroes
- Itinerant orators and chanters who go from mosque to mosque and home to home on special occasions
- Teachers in public schools and Quranic schools

The model for the *ulama* and their various roles is the prophet Muhammad. He was prophet, preacher, prayer leader, interpreter of the Quran, legal adviser and judge, teacher, counselor, and religious and political leader. A member of the *ulama* may act out several of these roles.

Ayatollah Khomeini of Iran was a famous member of the *ulama*. He studied for years under famous Islamic teachers. He published writings on Islam which affected a wide audience. He established theological schools. He taught many students whom he sent out to become leaders in mosques and Muslim communities. They gave loyalty and allegiance to him. As they spread, his teachings and influence inspired a revolution in Iran. His example inspired Islamic leaders in other nations.

Most members of the *ulama* serve in small mosques with small followings and with limited influence. They often have great influence upon the lives of Muslims who look to them in their communities. And most of them look to members of the *ulama* who are more experienced in matters of Islamic law, theology, and practice and seek their guidance.

FROM THIS LIFE TO THE NEXT

The straight path is set out in the Quran. Muslim beliefs and practices are commandments by God. They are not options to be debated. The practices are time-consuming; they occur regularly in the daily and monthly calendar; and they require commitment and energy to observe.

Although life is more than these essentials, Muslims believe that they are worshiping and obeying God in their performance and that their good deeds serve to balance the scales at the time of judgment and reward them with heaven. Love is little mentioned in the Quran, but obedience is mentioned a great deal. Obedience is the prerequisite for entrance into the garden of paradise.

The support system for Islam is the mosque community and the class of the *ulama* or clergy who give guidance and interpretation of the Quran, the hadith, and the law. Indeed, among Shiites there is a requirement that one select and engage a member of the *ulama* as one's mentor in all Islamic matters.

CHAPTER 5

A WHIRLWIND BEGINNING

A Global Expansion

WHY SO FAST?

No religion has spread so quickly and so far in its first one hundred years as Islam. From the hinterlands of the Arabian peninsula, it expanded eastward to the edges of China and westward through the Middle East and North Africa into Spain. Muslim empires ruled over vast populations.

The historic heart of Islam is in the Middle East. There are over one hundred million Arab Muslims. However, the strength of Islam goes far beyond its birthplace. India includes over one hundred million Muslims interspersed among its Hindu majority. There may be one hundred million Muslims in China. And Indonesia is the largest populated Muslim nation with over one hundred and eighty million Muslims, ninety percent of its population. Europe has over thirty million, and the United States has over five million Muslims, enabling Islam to challenge Judaism as the second-largest religion.

Islam emerged like a whirlwind. Following are some of the factors of its rapid advance:

- Social unrest in Mecca, Medina, and their environs
- An emerging movement toward monotheism
- A reaction against Hellenism in Syria and Egypt
- Decline of the Persian and Byzantine Empires

☪ Opportunities of Arab nomads to plunder neighboring lands
☪ Muhammad: prophet, reformer, warrior, administrator, strategist[1]

As Islam advanced, some populations converted to this religion of the straight path. Others were subdued and subjugated to the rule of Islam. There were some battles, and killings occurred. Some peoples, like Jews and Christians, were placed in minority status with the paying of taxes and with restrictions on some of their religious practices.

In some centuries, Islam was a reigning civilization. In others it was weak and in decline. The age of the crusades especially brought long-lasting tensions between Christianity and Islam. Since World War II, Islam has experienced revitalization and resurgence.

A BREAK FROM THE PAST

Tribalism, animism, and polytheism were dominant cultural patterns in pre-Islamic Arabia. A patriarchal society existed. Tribal warfare involved blood revenge and booty. Men had an unlimited number of wives and concubines.

Religion focused on the spirit world and on many deities, both male and female. The kaba housed various gods and goddesses. Sacrifices and offerings were made before the deities. Allah appeared to be a supreme god among many.

The Arabian peninsula was caught between two warring empires: the Byzantine Empire of Constantinople and the Sassanian Empire of Persia (Iran). Many tribes and peoples tired of warfare and looked for different leadership. Islam took advantage of this leadership vacuum.

Christianity was engaged in internal struggles between the Roman Catholic Church headquartered in Rome and the Eastern Orthodox Church headquartered in Constantinople. The issues focused on theological interpretations of the nature of God and the nature of Jesus Christ. Also, the polity of the church was at issue. Heresies were declared, and excommunications occurred. Islam arose amid Christian controversies and was influenced by these events.

MARRIAGES IN THE PENINSULA

Muhammad was born in Mecca in 570 within the Quraish tribe. Orphaned as a child, he married a wealthy widow merchant, Khadija, who was forty, at age twenty-five. This marriage gave him financial security and a wife who supported him during the turbulent times of his visions and preaching. He began receiving revelations in 610 from the angel Gabriel and was told to recite them.

His message was about one God, Allah, and his commandments. His message rejected tribal beliefs in spirits and deities. Muhammad gained several converts to his preaching, including Khadija, Ali his cousin, and Abu Bakr, who was later to become his father-in-law.

Because their lives were threatened, Muhammad and his followers fled to Medina. The flight to Medina in 622 marks the first year of the Islamic calendar. Certain tribal leaders in Medina, some two hundred miles to the north of Mecca, noticed Muhammad's qualities of leadership and determination. They invited him to come to Medina. His acceptance of these leaders' requests resulted in giving him a power base to realize the outcome of his revelations.

In Medina, he launched his formation of the Islamic community, the umma. He brought various tribes into Islam. Some tribes were subdued with great loss of life, including Jewish tribes who lost many of their men in battle with the Muslims.

Muhammad solidified his roles in Medina as prophet, ruler, judge, prayer leader, sermon giver, and commander in chief. By 629 he had captured Mecca and later cleansed the kaba and established it as the site of pilgrimage or haj.

By his death in Medina in 632, he was the ruling force in the peninsula and had set the pace of Islam to be a growing and powerful religious and political force in the world. He was buried in Medina, and the great mosque and his burial have become popular pilgrim places.

A SPLIT IN THE FAMILY

Prior to his death in 632, Muhammad did not officially designate a successor. He was the final prophet, but he also left a community of religious, political, legal, and military functions. His son-in-law Ali, married to Fatima, the prophet's daughter, urged the community to support him as successor to Muhammad.

The community refused and named Abu Bakr, an early convert, as the first leader or caliph. Ali's followers and kin did not agree with the decision. Omar and Uthman followed as the second and third caliphs. Ali later became the fourth caliph (656 to 661).

During the period of the caliphs, Muslims conquered Damascus (635), gained control of Iraq (636), and took Jerusalem (638). By 641 Egypt surrendered, and in 642 Persia came under Islamic control. A Persian slave assassinated Caliph Omar in 644, and discontented Muslims killed Caliph Uthman in 656.

The Shiite branch of Islam considered Ali not only the fourth caliph but also the first imam. The Shiites (*Shiite* means "partisan") had sought the successorship of Ali at the death of Muhammad. Ali had battles with Muawiya, the Sunni leader in Damascus, demonstrating the gravity split between the Shiites and Sunnis. A Kharijite tribesman assassinated Ali in 661. He left behind two sons, Hasan and Husain, who were to become the second and third imams in the Shiite tradition.

The Shiites grew to become the leading branch of Islam in Iran. Ali became a major figure of devotion in Shiite Islam. Husain, his son, also was to become a religious saint after whom mosques and tombs were named, religious plays were presented, and to whom prayers were offered. The profound division between Shiite and Sunni Islam is both theological and political.

The separation of the Shiites from the Sunnis did not hinder the growth and expansion of Islam. Islam spread like wildfire after the initial days of transition after the prophet's death. The Middle East became dominated with Islamic religion and rule. And North Africa and Europe as well as India and China were to be grounds of Islamic expansion.

ISLAM FROM EAST TO WEST

After 661, the Shiites sparred for leadership with the Sunnis. Hasan, Ali's son, ruled briefly as the Shiite's second imam. After he was poisoned, Husain, Ali's other prominent son, was named third imam. He battled the Umayyads, who had established their Sunni caliphate in Damascus. In 680 Husain and his entire family were brutally killed by Sunni forces in the battle of Kerbala in Iraq. They cut off his head and placed it on display in Damascus.

Husain's death has been memorialized by the Shiites in various gatherings and passion plays. Husain became a Shiite martyr and saint. His vicarious suffering and the shedding of his blood have become Shiite symbols and rituals of individual and community redemptive and revolutionary actions, especially during the season of Muharram.

The Umayyads had carried Islam across North Africa by 711. In that year the Muslim general Tariq invaded and dominated Spain. Gibraltar was named after him. In 732 the Muslim forces crossed the Pyrennes Mountains into France. In the Battle of Tours in France, Charles Martel led Christian armies against Muslim forces and defeated them. The Islamic advance into the heartland of Europe was stopped.

To the east of Arabia, Muslim forces pushed on to India and the fringes of China. Iran, Afghanistan, and Pakistan came under Islamic control. Even parts of central Asia were introduced to the prophet's teachings.

Thus Islam in its first one hundred years had gained ground all the way to Spain to the west and to the edges of China in the east. No other religion had made such an advance in such a brief time. Many peoples had accepted Islam as their new religion. Others had come under its political domination. Many were given minority status, especially Jews and Christians, to practice their mother religions under certain restrictions.

THE JEWELS OF ISLAMIC CIVILIZATION

Baghdad was the capital of the Abbasid Caliphate. The caliphate ruled a vast empire from 750 to 1258. These glorious years of Islamic civilization coincided with the so-called Dark Ages in Western Europe. There was a renaissance in literature, art, architecture, science, medicine, and education. Arabic was spoken from Spain to India. Muslim genius was shown in the building of the Alhambra in Grenada, Spain, to the Taj Mahal in Agra, India.

Islamic art is abstract. The designs take three forms: geometric, Arabesque, and calligraphic. The patterns are found on mosques, carpets, ceramic tiles, friezes, vases, lacquered boxes, and written portions of the Quran. The calligraphy of the Quran was most popular in the Bismillah ("In the Name of Allah, the Most Merciful, the Most Compassionate"), in the Shahada ("There is no God but God and Muhammad is the Prophet of God"), and in the Fatiha (the first chapter of the Quran). This was a way of praising God without picturing God.

Islamic architecture is seen most vividly in its mosques. Creative genius is displayed in the Red Fort in Delhi, the Alhambra in Grenada, and the Taj Mahal in Agra. Mosques have been called "calligraphy in architecture" and "theology in concrete."[2] Other examples of outstanding mosque architecture are the Arab-style mosque in Cordoba, the Turkish blue mosque in Istanbul, the Persian Shah mosque in Isfahan, and the Dome of the Rock in Jerusalem.

During the Abbasid Caliphate, Baghdad was a great intellectual center. Muslims excelled in physics, mathematics, and medicine. They invented the astrolabe, the pendulum, and the magnetic compass. The "x" was invented for an unknown quantity. They developed algebra and transmitted plane geometry and trigonometry to the West. After the zero was borrowed from India, a system of counting was developed known as Arabic numerals.

By 931 Baghdad had a fully staffed hospital and medical school with outpatient clinics, pharmacies, and libraries. Some 869 physicians took their medical exams at this time. Muslims used anesthesia in surgery and cauterized wounds. They developed the science of ophthalmology.

Al-Razi was considered the greatest physician in the Middle Ages. A Latin translation of his medical encyclopedia was the first medical book published in Europe.

Arabic prose and poetry were prominent during this time and influenced not only the Islamic world but also the West. The poems of Sadi, Hafez, and Rumi, *The Rubaiyat* of Omar Khayyam, and *A Thousand and*

Large mosque in Capetown, South Africa, funded by Muslim mission from the Middle East.

One Nights (known as *Arabian Nights*) are prominent examples of the literature of the period.

Al-Kindi (d. 873) was the first to translate Aristotle into Arabic. Ibn Sina (d. 1037), known as Avicenna in the West, fused philosophy and science with stress upon reason and religion. The great al-Ghazali defended revelation in religion by attacking the thought of Avicenna. Ibn Rushd (d. 1198), known as Averroes to the West, was profound in his knowledge of philosophy, mathematics, and medicine.

During this era, Sufism, a form of Islamic mysticism, gave vital spiritual energies and self-renewal to Islam. It emphasized the personal nature of God and a relationship with God based on emotions and love. Al-Ghazali and Rumi are noted Sufis. Rumi founded the Sufi brotherhood or order known as "whirling dervishes." Sufism became a missionary force which aided the expansion of Islam into Africa, Indonesia, Turkey, central Asia, and southern Europe.

Thus, the Abbasid Caliphate was a time of great flowering of Islamic civilization. From the prestigious university of al-Azhar in Cairo to the Islamic preservation in Arabic of the works of Plato and Aristotle, the medicine of Galen and Hippocrates, and the geometry of Euclid, the jewels of Muslim dominance shone with influence beyond their times.

THE CRUSADES NEVER TO BE FORGOTTEN

Soon after the death of Muhammad, Muslim armies captured Jerusalem and Palestine as they advanced westward. Beginning in 1099 and lasting into the thirteenth century, Christian armies under orders of the pope and European rulers, including Richard the Lionhearted of England, launched wars against the Muslim peoples of Jerusalem and Palestine. They became known as the Crusades.

The Christian armies had few successes for any length of time. Although they occupied Jerusalem for a spell, the Muslim general Saladin became famous by retaking the city in 1187.

The lands and the city remained under Islam until the establishment of the nation of Israel in 1948 through warfare between the Jews of Palestine and surrounding Muslim nations. Several other wars have occurred in the 1960s and 1970s between Israel and its Muslim neighbors, as well as strife with Muslim dissidents living in the state of Israel.

The repercussions of the Crusades are many. Muslims have viewed Christianity as a warring religion. They have believed that Christianity is a colonialistic, imperialistic, and political religion bent on dominating the world. Europe and the United States have been looked upon as Christian nations whose governments and foreign policies have been formulated to dominate Muslim societies politically, economically, culturally, and religiously.

Likewise, Muslims often view Christian missionaries as agents of Western imperialistic governments. There is great suspicion and distrust. The nation of Israel is seen as a further extension of the crusading mentality of the "Christian West" with its support of the United States and some European nations. During the Iranian revolution, the United States was called the "Great Satan" because of its support of the Shah of Iran, who was ousted by the preachments of Ayatollah Khomeini. The Islamic Republic of Iran was established to be the ideal Islamic nation with much antagonism toward Christianity and the Western nations.

Muslims still remember the Crusades, and they still distrust Western nations, Western cultures, and Christianity.

FROM THE OTTOMAN TURKS TO LAWRENCE OF ARABIA

By 1258 the Seljuk Turks had captured much of Syria from the crusaders. Baghdad fell to the Mongol Turk invaders in 1258, and the Abbasid caliph was assassinated. The Mongols took Syria. The Mamluk Turks established a caliphate in Cairo in 1261.

The Ottoman Turks captured Constantinople in 1453. By 1516 the Ottomans had defeated the Mamluks and had taken control of Syria and Palestine. Thus by 1517 the Ottomans had captured Cairo and ended the Mamluk dynasty.

In 1501 the Safavid dynasty gained control of Persia (Iran) and established Shiite Islam. The Shiites remained distinct in their practices of Islam. Emphasizing the imamate of the twelve imams, the leadership of the ayatollahs, and the rituals surrounding the family of Ali, especially his son Husain.

Various Turkish tribes invaded traditional Islamic lands. They became rulers and assimilated Muslim religious and political culture. They helped to fragment further the peoples and lands across the Middle East, Eastern Europe, and North Africa.

Constantinople became the capital of the Ottoman Empire. Its splendor was seen in the reign of Suleiman the Magnificent, the caliph from 1520 to 1566. France gained influence in the empire. On the other hand, Pope Pius V in 1571 organized the Holy League against the Ottomans. In 1638 the Ottomans took Baghdad from the Persians. By 1683 Christian armies turned back the Ottoman forces at the gates of Vienna.

The Ottoman Empire was in decline by the early 1700s. Muhammad Wahab began his ultraconservative movement of puritanical Islam in the Arabian peninsula. He was militant against corrupt Muslim leaders. His vision of Islam was a literal interpretation of the Quran and a return to the glory days of the prophet Muhammad.

Wahabbism was the forerunner of other similar movements of Islamic conservative resurgence, including the intellectuals like Afghani of Persia, Muhammad Abduh of Egypt, and Muhammad Rida of Syria.

Hasan Banna of Egypt and his disciple Sayyid Qubt (1906–1966) inspired and directed the formation of the Muslim Brotherhood. Qubt was executed by the Egyptian government for his radical teachings. Abul Mawdud (1903–1979) launched the Jamaat Islam in Pakistan.

In 1882 Great Britain invaded Egypt and controlled its affairs. By 1918, at the conclusion of World War I, the Ottoman Empire was on its last legs. Kemal Ataturk led the demise of Islam in Turkey. Known as the father of modernization, Ataturk pushed for secularism. Islamic jurisprudence, the power of the Muslim *ulama,* and Quranic schools were pushed aside. Secular values and institutions were initiated by the government.

The Arabs fought the empire, gained some independence, only to fall under European influence. Lawrence of Arabia portrayed the tensions of the times. Fighting for and with the Arab tribes for their political survival and land, the machinations of outside powers prevailed to dictate land boundaries and rulers.

The Ottoman Empire fell. Its seat of power, Istanbul, formerly Constantinople, became the focus of change from orthodox Islam to secularity. Islamic law, education, and culture faced the influences of Europeanization.

In Persia, the Shah of Iran, Reza Shah, emulated Ataturk's program and led the modernizing influences in Shiite Islam. Islam officially took second seat to the changes toward westernization. The later son of Reza Shah, Muhammad Reza Shah Pahlavi, was to continue his father's programs. Thus, Islamic orthodoxy among both Sunnis and Shiites was threatened by the forces which aided in the fall of the Ottoman Empire. But by 1979 resurgent conservative Islam under Ayatollah Khomeini overthrew the Shah and implemented the Islamic regime.

TWENTIETH-CENTURY ISLAM IN SICKNESS AND IN HEALTH

Muslims point to two idyllic eras of the fourteen hundred years of their religion. The first and always the primary period is the time of the prophet Muhammad and his founding of the first umma in Medina. Islam ruled in a theocratic state, and those who would not become Muslim submitted to its authority and rule.

The second era was the Abbasid Caliphate, the years of Islamic ascendancy and power (750–1268). It demonstrated the zenith of knowledge, intellectual pursuits, art and architecture, science and medicine, and the successful politics of power.

These two eras of Muslim prominence resonate in the minds and hearts of contemporary Muslims. The Quran and the hadith, the sayings and deeds of the prophet Muhammad, become even more the basis for thought and practice. With these dreams and paradigms, present-day Muslims work toward implementing the straight path.

The twentieth century began with the fall of the aging Ottoman Empire and the imperialism of Europe upon the fragmented Muslim populations. The twentieth century closed with the resurgence and revival of Islam across its heartland and into Africa, Southeast Asia, Central Asia, Europe, and the United States.

Key Dates in Islamic History

570	Muhammad born in Mecca
595	Muhammad marries wealthy widow Khadija
610	Beginning of Quranic revelation to Muhammad during Ramadan
622	Flight (Hegira) to Medina by Muhammad and followers to escape persecution and threats from Meccan tribes; first year of Islamic calendar
627	Muhammad and his forces execute seven to eight hundred Jews of the Bani Quraydha Jewish tribe
630	Mecca is occupied by Muslim forces
632	Muhammad performs the haj (pilgrimage) to Mecca in March Muhammad dies in June in Medina
635	Muslims conquer Damascus
636	Muslims conquer Iraq
638	Muslims conquer Jerusalem
641	Muslims conquer Egypt
642	Muslims conquer Persia (Iran)
652	Quran canonized
680	Husain, son of Ali and Fatima, and grandson of Muhammad, killed by Ummayad Muslim forces at Karbala, Iraq, and his head paraded in Damascus. Husain becomes martyred hero of Shiite Muslims
711	Islamic forces reach Spain
713	Muslims enter India
732	Islamic forces stopped in Battle of Tours in southern France
750–1258	Abbasid Caliphate headquartered in Baghdad with Islamic civilization excelling in art, architecture, science, medicine, philosophy
874	Twelfth Imam of Shiite Muslims disappears and goes into occultation. Shiites anticipate this Mahdi to return to restore justice and righteousness
1099	Christian Crusaders capture Jerusalem from Muslims
1187	Muslim General Saladin retakes Jerusalem from Crusaders
1453	Ottoman Turks conquer Constantinople
1517	Ottomans consolidate Ottoman Empire with control of Syria, Palestine, and Egypt
1536	Alliance between France and Ottoman Empire establishing French influence in region
1699	Ottoman expansion westward stopped and beginning of decline

1703	Birth of Muhammad ibn Wahhab in the Arabian Peninsula. Wahhab taught strict adherence to Islamic teachings and has served as inspiration to ultraconservative movements in Islamic world including the Muslim Brotherhood, Islamic Jihad, Hamas
1924	Turkey, the heartland of the Ottoman Empire, becomes a secular state
1979	Ayatollah Khomeini returns from exile to establish Islamic Republic of Iran after shah leaves country
1980	Iraq-Iran War begins
1990s	Various militant actions involving Muslim peoples in Eastern Europe, Middle East, Central Asia, Africa, including the countries of Afghanistan, Indonesia, Sudan
1990	U.S. Gulf War against Iraq with various alliances of Muslim nations
1993	PLO Leader Yasir Arafat and Israeli Prime Minister Rabin shake hands on plan for peace

SIX MAJOR FORCES ON ISLAM IN THE TWENTIETH CENTURY

Westernization

The heartland of the Middle East was invaded by outside forces, particularly those of Europe and the United States. Egypt, Algeria, Libya, Morocco, Palestine, Jordan, Syria, Lebanon, and Iraq were among the countries under control or influence by Great Britain, France, Italy, and the USSR. Iran was heavily influenced by Great Britain, the United States, and the USSR.

Outside powers gained entry through the League of Nations and, later, the United Nations, drawing partitions and boundaries through mandates, foreign aid, economic dependence, military advisors, and technological assistance. Muslims have gradually reacted to these influences.

As Islam moved beyond its heartland in the Middle East into Asia and Africa, it made adaptations to the major cultures of those areas. Thus cultures with dominant Hindu, Buddhist, animistic, and traditional tribal patterns often absorbed Islamic influence and patterns, if not dominance by Islam.

The Nation of Israel: A Thorn in the Muslim Flesh

The state of Israel was founded in 1948 within the background of the Balfour Declaration, the Sykes Agreement, and battles between the Jews and the Arabs of Palestine. The neighboring Arab nations waged the wars of 1947–48, 1952, 1967, and 1973 against Israel. Israel survived each war.

Islamic terrorist groups, including the PLO, Islamic Jihad, and Hamas, emerged, dedicated to destroy Israel. Muslims worldwide have rallied to the cause of repossession of Palestine and the Muslim holy sites in Jerusalem.

The conservative resurgence of Islam inspires jihad against the forces which founded and which support Israel and against Israel itself. Jerusalem and Palestine have become a central focus among worldwide Muslims, uniting them above nationality and religious sectarianism.

Nationalism among Muslim Leaders

In reaction to Western colonialism and ultraorthodox Islam, some predominantly Muslim nations have attempted governance on nationalistic and socialistic principles. These efforts have been, in part, an attempt to relate their nations to modern politics, economics, and international relations.

Some nations have succeeded. Some have had to battle dissident Muslims who want Islam to be the principle law and order of the nation. Some have continued relations with the colonialist outside powers. Some have sought assistance from countries not aligned with the West.[3]

Egypt and Syria are examples of nations whose governments have looked to change in the social order while attempting respect for Islam. Indonesia at its founding as a modern state incorporated the freedom of religion for all, even though its population was predominantly Muslim. However, these three nations have faced internal turmoil in the clash of traditional Islam and social change.

Oil—an Islamic Blessing and Curse

Oil-wealthy Muslim-dominated nations, including Saudi Arabia, Iran, and Iraq, began to nationalize their oil resources in the 1960s. They soon began collecting the lion's share of oil profits formerly controlled by Europe and the United States.

Oil was a curse to Islam. Muslim nations used their new wealth to modernize, but modernization left them dependent on the West for technology and skills. Modernization weakened Islamic values and institutions. Soon the most conservative Muslims dissented and rebelled. The most important upheaval occurred in Iran when Ayatollah Khomeini deposed the Western-leaning Shah.

But oil was also a blessing to Islam. Oil money enabled Muslim nations to export Islam around the globe. With more money, they sent Muslim missionaries to Africa, Central Asia, Europe, and the United

States, carrying Qurans, building mosques, and establishing Islamic schools and libraries and associations.

Islamic Republic of Iran: The Turban and the Crown

The Shah of Iran had held power since the early 1950s as Shahenshah, "king of kings." He was a favorite son of United States foreign policy. He had continued his father Reza Shah's policies of modernization and the containment of Shiite Islam. He had helped shield the Soviet Union from the Persian Gulf oil wealth, which the West monopolized.

Dissent became so great against the Shah that Ayatollah Khomeini overthrew him and established the Islamic Republic of Iran in 1979. Khomeini attempted to govern by the principles of the Quran and the prophet Muhammad.

Iran began to export Islam to faraway places and became the premier Muslim missionary nation. Iran and its revolution became a model for worldwide Muslims who wanted a return to the glory days of Islam.

Significant Growth and Influence: Still Counting

Islam now has more than one billion followers. It is not only birthrate growth but also intentional missionary growth. It is growing in nations of over 100 million populations. It is growing in Western nations not only in numbers but also in influence and power. It is the second-largest religion in Europe and emerging as such in the United States.

Several general patterns emerge when the history of Islamic growth and expansion are observed.

- Muhammad promoted a precise worldview and program that were cohesive and meaningful to his followers.
- The leaders of Islam did not hesitate to use force and violence to extend the religion.
- Differences over leadership and governance emerged early among Muslims.
- Violence and killings and wars between Muslims have existed to the present.
- Islam has feuded with Christianity since its inception.
- Islam created grand civilizations and empires.
- Islam has long had a love-hate relationship with Western governments and cultural values.
- Jihad, a holy war, has been a viable and threatened and expressed action through the centuries of Islam.

✻ Factionalism and schism continue to mark the house of Islam.

✻ Opposition to Zionism and the right to reclaim Jerusalem have unified Muslims worldwide.

✻ Muslims exhibit unceasing missionary effort toward non-Muslims.

Islam began like a whirlwind in the Arabian Peninsula and has since spread like wildfire across the globe. There are over one billion Muslims. Asia has over 775 million, Africa over 300 million, Latin America over 1.3 million, and Oceania over 385,000. There are over thirty million in the heartland of Europe with over five million in North America.

Forty-three percent of the world's Muslims live in four countries: Indonesia (170 million), Pakistan (118 million), India (106 million), and Bangladesh (103 million). Islam is growing and counting.

CHAPTER 6

ARE ALL MUSLIMS ALIKE?

Unity and Diversity

MUCH UNITY

The Brotherhood of Islam

Islam is characterized by unity. The prophet Muhammad began Islam by establishing the brotherhood of Muslims in lieu of the disunity of the tribes of the Arabian peninsula. Every Muslim, regardless of nationality, language, or political persuasion, believes the tenets and practices of the pillars of the faith. Every Muslim believes what is written in the Quran. All Muslims must honor the life and character of their prophet.

Unity, Uniformity, and Universality

God is one. He sends angels. Prophets speak his message. There are sacred scriptures. A judgment day is coming, and one will go either to heaven or hell. Gabriel brought the perfect revelation from God in heaven to Muhammad. Muhammad is the last prophet. The Quran is the perfect embodiment of God's laws and commandments. Any other scriptures, including the Bible, have been corrupted and must be judged in light of the Quran.

Muslims are united in observing these pillars of their faith. The Quran says so. They must voice the confession and say the prayers daily in Arabic, even though their native language may not be Arabic. They must pray five times daily facing Mecca. They must fast every year during Ramadan. They must save their money to make the once-in-a-lifetime pilgrimage to Mecca so they may become a *haji*, as those who have made the pilgrimage are known. They must give a percentage of their goods and income to promote Islam. They must practice jihad.

The lunar calendar unites individual religion with that of the community, with Islamic events, ceremonies, and festivals. The mosque is a place of worship, prayer, and fellowship, though Muslims are not required to go to the mosque. Many do go to the mosque from early childhood until their death. In traditional societies, families solemnize marriages there, seal business deals, and even plot political mischief.

Muslims are also unified in their belief about Jesus and the Bible. They accept what the Quran says: that Jesus was a prophet, that he was born of the virgin Mary, that he did not die on the cross, that he was a man but not the Son of God who died for the sins of the world. They believe that the Jewish and Christian scriptures have been corrupted over time from their original perfect revelation and that the Quran corrects what the Bible incorrectly reports.

Muslims are united in their zeal to regain the rights of Palestinians to their land. The Islamic holy places must be retained and controlled by its own authorities.

Unity, uniformity, and universality characterize Islam. Muslims unite around the infallibility and veracity of the Quran and the exemplary life and teachings of Muhammad. Their practices of the pillars are regular and unchanging. And they believe they have the superior religion, which should be extended universally across the globe.

MUCH DIVERSITY

Muslims may hold in great unity and with much tenacity to the major beliefs and pillars of their religion, yet these same Muslims may differ greatly with one another. The differences may be affected by politics, legal interpretations, theological positions, and cultural variations.

Several major Islamic legal traditions were in place during the first several centuries. One legal tradition may interpret and rule a harsher penalty for a violation of Islamic law than another. Some Muslim societies imprison thieves; others cut off one of their hands.

Another example revolves around a theological-political disagreement. At the prophet Muhammad's death, he left no will or direction as to who would succeed him. One group, the Sunnis, said his successor should be elected by the Muslim community. Another group, the Shiites, said his successor should be a member of the prophet's family. A schism developed and has lasted.

When Islam crosses cultures, it may accommodate to certain values of the culture or that culture may add some of its values to its interpretation of Islam. An example is the veneration or worship of saints. Some Muslims voice prayers to saints and pray at the tombs of saints. Muhammad condemned this practice, and orthodoxy does the same.

Diversity among Muslims includes the following:

- Four major schools of Islamic law
- Sectarian groups like Sunni, Shiite, Sufi, Wahhabi, Ahmadiyya, Nation of Islam, Muslim Brotherhood
- High profile leaders of Islamic nations
- Leaders of militant Islamic groups
- Folk Islam

FOUR SCHOOLS OF ISLAMIC LAW

Islamic law (*sharia*) is primary to the community. It is based on the following:

- Quran: the revealed and perfect word of Allah
- Hadith: the traditions about the life and sayings of Muhammad
- Ijma: the consensus of the community under the leadership of the *ulama*
- Qiyas: analogical reasoning and deduction by *ulama* based on the other three sources

A class of Islamic scholars and jurists called *ulama* make interpretations of the law. These jurists developed schools of law. Each school may make decisions about matters such as marriage rights, divorce procedures, inheritance, and forms of punishment, which may differ from each other.

Four major schools of law are Shafite, Hanafite, Malikite, and Habalite.

- Shafite school was founded by al Shafi, who died in 820. This school is known for its classical theory of Islamic law based on proper prophetic tradition with the use of analogical reasoning for applications to new circumstances.
- Hanafite school was founded by Abu Hanafah in Iran in the eighth century. More freedom is allowed in interpretation, and it is considered one of the more liberal legal traditions.

🕮 Malikite school was founded by Malik Ibn Anas in Medina. He died in 795. He relied on the living tradition of Medina as supported by the hadith.

🕮 Hanbalite is the latest school begun by Ahmad ibn Hanbal, who died in 855. Its interpretations of the Quran are very legalistic and literalistic. It is the dominant school in Saudi Arabia.

THE SUNNI ORTHODOX

Ninety percent of all Muslims are Sunni. The Sunni represent the orthodoxy or tradition of Islam. They adhere to the major beliefs and observe the pillars of the faith. Their strong stand is on the succession to Muhammad. They teach that the successor to the prophet Muhammad should be a male from the Quraish tribe to which he belonged.

The leader should be selected by consensus (ijma) of the community. He should be a caliph given the responsibility to govern following the Quran and the traditions of the prophet.

Beginning with Abu Bakr in 632, caliphs have ruled according to the *sharia* law. The caliphate was disbanded in 1924 when the Ottoman Empire fell. Various Islamic nations include some degree of the Islamic law in their cultural patterns and administration of justice. Noted members of the *ulama*, bearing various titles such as imam or sheik, are recognized for their scholarly and legal acumen and are called upon to give counsel and interpretations of *sharia*.

Sunnis and Shiites have had differences since the death of Muhammad. Shiites remember with disgust and hatred the slaughter of Husain, the grandson of prophet Muhammad, and his family at Kerbala, Iraq, and his beheading by the Sunni army. At their best moments, Sunnis and Shiites consider themselves brothers and sisters in the religion. And though ideally they may pray and worship together in the mosque, theological and political differences are so great that most often they have separate communities with mosques, rituals, and leaders.

THE SHIITE REFORMERS

The Shiite faction began shortly after the death of Muhammad. *Shiite* means "partisan," and the object of Shiite partisanship or favoritism is to Ali, the son-in-law of Muhammad.

Shiite traditions relate that Muhammad said that those who look to him as master will also look to Ali. What Aaron was to Moses was what Ali was to Muhammad. Thus they strongly believe that Muhammad invested Ali with the mantel of leadership to be his successor. Ali came to be known as having the qualities of sinlessness in leadership and infallibility in interpreting the Quran.

According to Shiite tradition, succession was to remain in the family of the prophet. Ali was to be the first imam and to establish the imamate. His sons were to continue the leadership. Ali was denied this status. The Muslim community instead selected Abu Bakr as the first caliph.

Ali was selected the fourth caliph. Shiites consider him the first imam. He placed his relatives in administrative posts. Conflict ensued. He was murdered and buried in Najaf, Iraq. His tomb has been a great Shiite shrine. It is believed that a pilgrimage to the shrine merits the rewards of 100,000 martyrdoms and the forgiveness of both present and past sins.

Hasan, Ali's first son, was proclaimed caliph (second imam). However, there was rivalry between Hasan and Muawiya. Muawiya forced Hasan to abdicate. Hasan retired to Medina with his sixty wives, where he was poisoned. Muawiya reigned as Sunni caliph in Damascus.

Husain, Ali's second son, made an attempt to become imam and supplant Muawiya. He and his family and friends were slaughtered by the Sunni army, led by Yazid the son of Muawiya, at Kerbala, Iraq, in 680 on the tenth day of the Muslim month of Muharram. His head was taken to Damascus, and his body was trampled under the hoofs of horses.

The tenth of Muharram has gone down as a day of infamy. Shiite animosity toward the Sunnis has been commonplace. Husain's tomb at Kerbala has become a Shiite shrine. According to tradition, a pilgrimage there merits the value of a thousand pilgrimages to Mecca, a thousand martyrdoms, and a thousand days of fasting.

Husain is a martyr. His murder has become a distinct feature of Shiite faith and practice. The shedding of his blood has sacrificial and vicarious value. Each year during the month of Muharram, narratives, sermons, and passion plays in mosques, homes, and parades tell the story. They tell of and enact the gruesome details of the deaths of Husain and his family, including the little children. Men clothe themselves in white, beat their heads and chests with chains, and draw blood to stain the white garments.[1]

These enactments demonstrate mourning, purging of one's soul, identifying with Husain's fight against evil, and supplication for his power to aid them against evil and injustice.

Shiite doctrine teaches that there were twelve imams. The twelfth imam went into hiding in 870. He will return at an appropriate time as the Mahdi and overcome evil and injustice and restore righteousness. Until his return, Shiites believe that an ayatollah may rule in his stead.

Iran is the leading Shiite nation with this understanding of Islam and with the power of an ayatollah.

Shiites believe in the imamate versus the caliphate. They have elevated the prophet's family to leadership with spiritual and infallible qualities. They believe in spiritual power associated with hero tombs, like Ali and Husain. The imamate is of such importance that they add to the orthodox Islamic confession (*shahada*) a phrase that declares Ali the commander of true believers and the friend of God.

THE SUFI MYSTICS

Sufism is Islamic mysticism. Sufis believe the soul can rise through prayer and discipline to the very presence of God to be united with him. They read the Quran as an allegory of the soul's quest for union with God. They follow the inward path (*Tariqa*) of religion, the path of love.

The practice of Sufism cuts across much of Islam. Some Muslims may be Sunni or Shiite and still appreciate Sufism. The word *sufi* comes from a word meaning "purity" and "wool." It has roots in asceticism. Early ascetics wore white garments and withdrew from society. They protested the worldliness of the Muslim princes in Damascus and sought a direct experience with God apart from formal rituals.

Sufis sought God through introspection and inward experiences. They believed that God was closer than the jugular vein. They thought of God as a light shining and burning within the soul. Sufis interpret Muhammad's miraculous night journey to heaven to see God face to face.

Through the ages prominent Sufis have established their schools and brotherhoods. Al-Hallaj even claimed that he was ultimate reality. He was executed by crucifixion in 922. The famous scholar, al-Ghazali, sought to reconcile orthodoxy and mysticism. After having a personal encounter with God, he taught that the love of God rather than union with God is central to religion. He has been called the Thomas Aquinas of Muslim theology.

Al-Din Rumi founded the Sufi order known as the "whirling dervishes." They repeat the name of God as they dance to music. Often shrines were built in veneration to Sufi leaders called sheiks. The sheik became a saint, and Sufis believed they could have communion with the saint because of his holiness and closeness to God. A famous Sufi brotherhood found in many parts of the world is the Quadiriya.

The Sufi brotherhoods are the most aggressive missionary organizations of Islam. Islam in Indonesia, parts of Africa and Asia, and in Europe finds its roots in Sufi Muslims establishing their faith.

WAHHABISM: ULTRAORTHODOX ISLAM

Al Wahhab (d. 1787) founded a Muslim puritan movement in Saudi Arabia known as Wahhabism. It follows the Sunni tradition of the Hanbali legal school. The Wahhabis are literalists in Quranic interpretation. The golden age of the time of the prophet and the first caliphs are its exemplary models of Islam.

If the Quran says God has hands and feet, they accept it. They say prayers daily in the mosque using only the words of the Quran. The Quranic penal law of beheading and the severing of hands for the designated crimes are meted out. They condemn idol and saint worship, especially that associated with the tombs of saints. They despise Sufism.

Jihad has been a frequent tool of the movement to condemn its enemies with threats, including both Muslims and non-Muslims. It has aggressively condemned Westernization and its acceptance by Muslim peoples.

Modern-day Saudi Arabian rulers are heirs of the legacy of Al Wahhab's teachings. In their thirst for modernization and corresponding dependence on Western nations, the Saud dynasty has been criticized and attacked by Wahhabi leaders. The rulers have attempted to moderate its influence.

However, Wahhabism has been strong in preventing Christian influences into the country. There is no admission of Christian missionaries or the building of churches. No non-Muslim is allowed to enter the environs of the city of Mecca. Wahhabism has had deep influence upon other ultraconservative Islamic movements in worldwide Islam.

FARRAKHAN'S NATION OF ISLAM

The Nation of Islam began among blacks in the United States in the 1930s. Elijah Poole, a Baptist from the South, was introduced in Detroit to W. D. Fard of whose background little is known. Fard introduced Elijah to a syncretistic Islam that combined racist teachings with Islamic vocabulary and occult mysticism. Elijah brought to the mix his own Christian background. He changed his name to Elijah Muhammad and launched his movement.

A central belief was that blacks were the first of creation, that whites were devils, and that the black race was to gain its rightful leadership when God destroys the white race. Elijah preached that Christianity was the white man's religion. He referred to God as Allah, to the Quran as the holy book, and to himself as prophet.

Several million American blacks joined the Islamic movement from the 1930s through the 1970s. They attended mosques open only to black members. Guards known as the Fruit of Islam provided security at the mosque doors. Elijah's dream was to provide for his followers a land of their own, either outside the United States or in its southland.

Elijah tolerated no dissent. He reprimanded anyone who tended to question his teachings. He knew little of the intricacies of Islam and used little Arabic in prayers or addresses. He came to view his mentor, W. D. Fard, as Allah in the flesh. After his own death, Elijah himself was to be considered by Louis Farrakhan as Allah in the flesh.

Elijah's son, Wallace Muhammad, succeeded him at his death in 1975, but the movement was divided in Elijah's later years. Malcolm X, a rising star under Elijah, veered closer to orthodox Islam and began to attack Elijah's syncretistic teachings and marital infidelities. Malcolm X was murdered by dissident Muslims as he spoke at a meeting in Harlem in 1965.

Wallace also decried his father's philandering and his unorthodox Islamic teachings. His father had dismissed him from the movement several times. After Elijah's death, Wallace turned the Nation of Islam toward orthodoxy, changed its name to the American Muslim Mission, and became recognized as a sound Muslim leader throughout the Islamic world. He introduced the readily acceptable beliefs and practices of Quranic Islam.

As Wallace moved toward orthodox Islam, Louis Farrakhan vowed to continue the tradition of Elijah Muhammad in the Nation of Islam. By 1985 Wallace disbanded the American Muslim Mission. He continued to assume the mantel of leadership of orthodox black Muslims in America.

With funding from Islamic countries abroad, Wallace had launched the building of Islamic centers, educational programs, and business ventures for black Muslims. He had accepted the invitation to give the invocation to open the United States Senate in the name of Allah. Now international Islam and American political leaders welcomed Wallace Muhammad. He gained a place of leadership within mainstream American religion which he had never had in the Nation of Islam.

Conversely, Louis Farrakhan moved further from orthodox Islam. His Nation of Islam continued to maintain its separatist and racist views and programs. He accepted invitations to visit Islamic-ruled nations such as Libya and Iran. He organized and spearheaded the Million-Man March to Washington, D.C., in 1995. However, Farrakhan remained controversial in statements about policies of the United States government, about Christianity, and about Judaism and the Jews.

Farrakhan's brand of Islam continued the major tenets of his mentor Elijah Muhammad, which include the following:

There is one God Allah. The Quran and the truth of the Bible are to be believed, though the present Bible is corrupt and must be reinterpreted. Allah's prophets and their scriptures must be accepted. The judgment of Allah will take place first in America. Black and white Americans should be separated now. Integration is hypocritical and deceptive. Allah appeared in the person of Master W. Fard Muhammad in July 1930. Fard was the Christian Messiah and the Muslim Mahdi.

FOLK ISLAM

A Muslim may affirm all the orthodox beliefs and practices of the required pillars of Islam and still deviate from the Quran. For various theological and cultural reasons, Muslims may emphasize local customs and heartfelt needs that change or add to orthodoxy. This is called popular or informal or folk Islam.

The further away Islam is from its epicenter, Mecca, and from its traditional Arabic culture, the more it may be affected by different cultures and languages. The following examples may illustrate folk Islam.

- Shiite Muslims highly venerate the prophet Muhammad's family.[2] They build shrines named after Ali, Husain, and others of the twelve imams. Prayers are offered in their names. They speak of Husain's sacrificial suffering and of their vicarious participation in his death and martyrdom. In contrast, orthodox Sunni Islam prays only to Allah and decries saint veneration.
- Sufism has received the wrath of orthodox Islam since its inception. Sufis have emphasized the presence and love and closeness of God in saying that God is closer than the jugular vein. Through their dancing and music, they demonstrate the strong emotional and personal side of religion and experience the nearness of God. This is a reaction against orthodoxy's distant and unfeeling God.
- Orthodoxy has maintained that Muhammad was only a prophet and human being and is not to be venerated. Folk Islam, while accepting him as final prophet, gives him a personal place in the Muslim's devotional life. Mosques are named after him. His figure may appear on the dashboard of taxis for protection in the hazards of driving. Other prophets of Islam, such as Moses and Jesus, have shrines named after them. Supplications are offered to some prophets, including Jesus. Thus, folk Islam expresses the need for a personal mediator who hears prayers and who may personally act on behalf of believers.

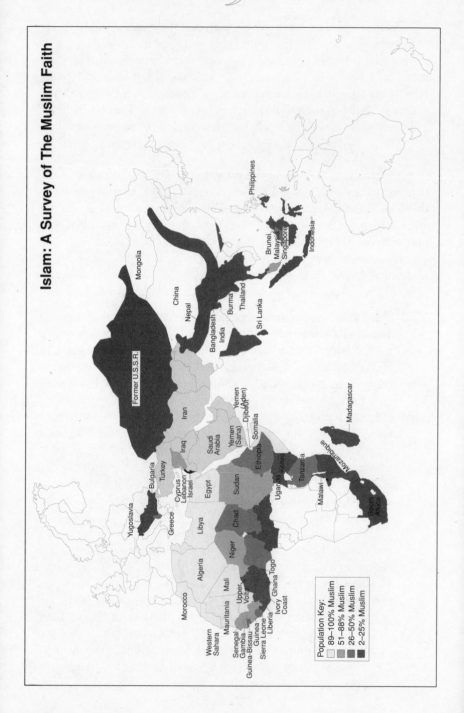

Islam: A Survey of The Muslim Faith

Population Key:
89–100% Muslim
51–88% Muslim
26–50% Muslim
2–25% Muslim

🕌 Across the Islamic world, most of the more than one billion followers will never make the pilgrimage to Mecca in their lifetime. Other pilgrim places and tombs become substitutions for Mecca because they are nearer and because they represent a local tradition. Many tombs of saints across the Middle East, North Africa, and sub-Sahara Africa provide merits for pilgrimages.

🕌 As has been noted, the tombs of Ali and Husain in Iraq provide Shiites with rewards sufficient to gain heaven. Although Mecca remains the ideal haj, these other places become more popular and bring religious satisfaction to many.

🕌 Calligraphy of the Quran has been the trademark of orthodoxy in art and architecture. Folk Islam allows pictures of prophets and saints. These are displayed in homes, shops, and saints' tombs and shrines. The orthodox consider these displays a desecration.

Thus, folk Islam is widespread among world Muslims. It uses fetishes, amulets, pictures and relics, prayers in the name of saints and heroes, and pilgrimages to saints' tombs. It appears to speak to the hearts and from the hearts of Muslims. It gives attention to the emotional and personal side of religion. It honors sages and often attributes more than human traits to them.

Folk religion is an addition to mainstream Islam. A Muslim may state the confession, may go to the mosque for the five stated prayers in the Arabic language, may observe the fasting season Ramadan, and may even make the pilgrimage to Mecca. The same Muslim may practice many of the ways of folk Islam. Perceiving these popular expressions as challenges and criticisms, orthodox Islam disparages and condemns folk Islam.

OTHER DIVISIONS WITHIN ISLAM

The history of Islam chronicles many sectarian divisions. Although the Sunni and Shiite separation has been the most prominent, many others have occurred.

Two major schools of theology developed. The Mutazilites were founded by Wasil ibn Ata (d. 749). This school emphasized reason as a final arbiter in matters of faith. Human freedom and responsibility were taught over against predestination. Another school, the Asharites, was begun by Ali ibn al Ashari (d. 935). It taught that revelation was the final arbiter in issues of faith. It stood for predestination over against human freedom.

Several Shiite sects developed. The largest and most famous is the Twelvers, who stand upon the twelve imams and the imamate as their leaders. Ali and Hasain are the most noted of the twelve with the twelfth imam as the Mahdi. The Mahdi is the "hidden imam" who will return at the end of the world. Iran is founded on this Shiite sect.

The Ismailis are another Shiite sect. They are often called the Seveners because they consider Ismail, the seventh imam, the last one. The Ismailis as a group are most numerous in Pakistan and India. Spin-offs from the Ismaili sect over time are the Fatimids of Egypt, the Druze (primarily located in Palestine), and the Assassins, known as the terrorists of the twelfth and thirteenth centuries. They were primarily located in Syria.

The Ahmadiyya sect was founded in India by Mirza Ghulam Ahmad, who proclaimed himself the returned Mahdi in 1889. The Ahmadis believe that Ahmad received revelations from God, that he is the returned imam or Mahdi, and that his mission is to purify Islam and convert the world to Islam. The Ahmadiyya are an aggressive worldwide missionary movement. Orthodox Islam has long criticized the movement as heretical.

Islam in America also has many faces. Besides the orthodoxy represented by Wallace Muhammad and millions of American Muslims, there are various groups. Perhaps the most prominent sect is the Nation of Islam under Louis Farrakhan. Others include Ansuru Allah, Nubian Islamic Hebrews, the Hanafi, the Islamic Party of North America, United Submitters International, and the American Druze Society.

There is much unity in Islam. Unity is particularly centered in the central beliefs enunciated in the Quran and in the examples in the life and teachings of the prophet Muhammad. However, there is much disunity. Sectarianism developed based on various theological interpretations of the Quran and the hadith, on political realities, and on cultural syncretism. Sectarianism and divisions have not limited Islam from growing and expanding to a worldwide religion with greater similarities than differences.

CHAPTER 7

SITTING AT TABLE
WITH MUSLIMS

CLUES TO UNDERSTANDING AND HOSPITALITY

Muslims live in almost all major cultural areas of the globe. They travel widely. They take up residence outside their home countries. They marry non-Muslims and raise their families in Islam. They study in universities around the world. They carry their religion with them and need places of prayer and association with other Muslims.

Those who meet Muslims need certain information to facilitate cordiality and hospitality. Although all Muslims regardless of nationality and language will observe the basic teachings of the Quran regarding behavior, there will be some differences among them. These differences may be based on theological interpretations, cultural variations between, say, an African Muslim and one from the Middle East, and from diverse practices of Islamic law or *sharia*. One needs to know enough of Islam and its cultural ways to greet and meet Muslims with respect and sensitivity.

If a Muslim brings a gift upon visitation in one's home, it is generally expected for one to reciprocate when visiting the Muslim home.

Muslims deeply appreciate friendships with non-Muslims. Three significant occasions where friendship is expressed are at the birth of a child, at a wedding of a family member, and at the death and burial of a loved one. Not only to understand the rituals on these occasions but also to be sensitive in one's presence is to greet and meet Muslims in cordiality and hospitality. Of course, the exchanges of visits between homes around meals are times for great fun and fellowship. To know what foods to prepare and what content of conversations to pursue is most helpful.

OLD WAYS, NEW TIMES

The traditional family arrangement has been one of a man with several wives, many children, the extended family living together, the man as the breadwinner, and the women as the home builders. Children were educated by the *ulama* in Quranic schools, and the *sharia* law governed family and domestic matters.

Modern times have challenged the family structure. Western legal codes have often supplanted *sharia* law. Western culture in the forms of educational curricula, dress, and technology has been assimilated into Muslim life. The old ways of Islamic life have faced new times. Women have received more education and have become breadwinners and gained more rights outside the home. The women's dress veil has been discarded.

The transition from tradition to modernity has created great stress among many Muslim peoples. Women in Saudi Arabia protested against the prohibition of their having driving licenses. Women in Iran protested against the required veiling by the Islamic Republic. The Afghanistan ruling authorities forced women out of public education and public work back into domestic chores. However, some Muslim societies have relished the preservation of their traditions and lamented the intrusions of outside values.

THE FAMILY

The family is central to Islamic life and community. (Quran 66:6) Traditionally, large families are enjoyed with parents, grandparents, children, and grandchildren living close by and socializing frequently. The males usually have prominence in the public domain while females tend to have greater responsibilities in the home.

Parents often help their children in vocational decisions and in securing a mate. Children are expected to care for their parents as they age. Generally, males and females are segregated in public life and in religious activities such as the prayers at the mosque. One's family is the source of honor and reputation. Women are restricted and protected by Islamic law and custom. In particular, the behavior of women reflects upon their family's honor.

Extramarital sex is illegal and prohibited. Brothers protect their sisters. Husbands protect their wives. In fact, a man's honor is based on how well he protects the women in his care.

MARRIAGE AND DIVORCE

It is stated in the Quran and reported by the prophet Muhammad that a Muslim has perfected half of his religion when he marries. He is cautioned to be God-fearing and careful with the other half. The Quran says that God created mankind from one living soul, and from that soul a spouse was created so that man might find comfort in her. (4:1; 7:107) Thus asceticism is not encouraged.

Muhammad said that a man should seek a wife for her wealth, beauty, and the nobility of her stock. But primarily a wife should be sought for her piety. Whatever dowry the man gave his bride-to-be and whatever she had before and after the wedding belonged to her.

Marriage was intended to be permanent. Muhammad condemned men and women who frequently changed marriage partners and described divorce as the most detestable of all lawful things before God. However, provisions were made for divorce. (Quran 2:228–241) Traditionally, a husband could divorce a wife by reciting before witnesses three times, "I divorce you." In modern Islamic societies, various laws prescribe the rules of divorce and the benefits of each party.

POLYGAMY

A major stereotype of Islam is that it allows a man to have many wives. It is true that the Quran permits a man to have up to four wives under certain conditions. It is a conditional permission and not a matter of necessity. A prerequisite of polygamy is for the wives to have the same rights and privileges. The Quran insists that they be treated justly. (4:3; 4:129)

Although the Quran and tradition demonstrate that polygamy was not only permitted but practiced, it is not the rule of thumb in modern times. Many Islamic nations prohibit it; others control it. And individual economics and social conditions affect a man's choice to have only one wife.

HUSBAND AND WIFE

Marriage roles for men and women are highly specific in Islam. Husbands are trustees and protectors of wives. The Quran states that God has made men to excel over others and to expend of their means. (2:228; 4:34) Muslim scholars interpret *excel* and *expend* as a division of labor and different roles. According to them, it does not mean the superiority of one gender over the other.

The wife must have sexual intimacy only with her husband. She must prepare herself to be attractive and to be responsive to her husband

and not deny intimacy with him. She must not deceive her husband in avoiding contraception in order to have children. She cannot entertain strange men without the consent of her husband.

THE PROPHET MUHAMMAD AND HIS WIVES

The Quran made an exception for the prophet Muhammad in the number of wives he might have. God assigned Muhammad the choices of the wives of the prisoners of war, the daughters of his paternal uncles and aunts, the daughters of his maternal uncles and aunts, and any believing woman who dedicated herself to him and whom he wished to marry. (Quran 33:50)

He had nine to thirteen wives and/or concubines. He married Khadija when he was twenty-five and she forty. After her death he married widows and divorcees. He married Aisha, the young daughter of Abu Bakr, an early convert and first caliph. Aisha was six years old at the time of the betrothal and nine when they consummated the marriage. Tradition indicates she was his favorite wife for the last nine years of his life.

Much discussion has ensued about the motives and relationships of Muhammad's sex life and marriages. Some suggest that he married for political alliances to make the Islamic community stronger; for diplomatic purposes; to take care of widows and orphans; and for sexual attractions and needs. Muhammad also had female captives to whom he had sexual rights.

Tradition indicates that Muhammad was given the strength of thirty men in his relations with his wives.[1] He visited each one regularly in their separate residences. However, his favoritism with young Aisha caused problems and jealousies. The other wives sent Fatima, his daughter, to ask him to spend equal time with each wife. Muhammad responded that revelations came to him when he was in bed with Aisha but not when with the others. He asked them to love Aisha and basically to accept things as they were.

The hadith or traditions of the sayings and deeds of Muhammad describe the attitudes and relationships of Muhammad toward women and toward his wives. He was a lover, a provider, and an arbiter between his wives. There were times of harmony and times of disharmony in his married life.

Muslims accept these traditions with his wives as truthful and authoritative. These traditions add information beyond the Quran on polygamy as well as the status of women. The behavior of Muhammad in the authoritative hadith is without question and has been exemplary for Muslims. However, modern Muslim societies have limited and controlled polygamy through legislation and education.

THE VEILING OF WOMEN

The veiling and seclusion of women have been a part of Muslim life across cultures. The Quran enjoined the prophet to tell his wives and daughters, as well as the wives of true believers, to draw veils close around them. The veil would allow them to be recognized but not molested. (Quran 33:59)

Muhammad told his followers that women should lower their eyes in public. They should not display their beauty and ornaments. Wear the veil and show beauty only to their husbands, he commanded. Thus, the veiling of women became a matter of honor, dignity, purity, and chastity.

Muslim cultures have different customs with regard to the veil. In Saudi Arabia, for example, a traditional Muslim woman will wear a floor-length black robe and a black veil over her head and face in public to be modest according to the Quran and to avoid the lustful looks of men. In other countries a woman may maintain a modest appearance by covering shoulders, arms, and legs. In Indonesia, the largest populated Muslim country, most women go unveiled. In his Turkish reform program of 1924, Kemal Ataturk forbade women to wear the veil. More recently, Reza Shah in Iran also prohibited wearing the veil.

Thus, the veiling and segregation of women have taken different forms over the history of Islam. Women have used the veil or appropriate clothing according to the interpretations made of the Quran and the traditions by the ruling clergy and political leaders of the times.

By the time of al-Rashid 150 years after the death of Muhammad, the haram system of seclusion was in place. Women of the richer classes were secluded from the household and tended by eunuchs. Tradition has kept women separated from men during prayers in the mosque.

The status of women in general in Islam is a subject of much interest. The Quran indicates that men are to be the protectors and maintainers of women and that women are to be devoutly obedient to their husbands. If wives demonstrate disloyalty and ill conduct, husbands are directed first to admonish them, second not to sleep with them, and third to beat them lightly. If wives become obedient, husbands are to accept them without punishments. (Quran 4:34) Wives are subject to the control of their husbands. (Quran 2:223)

Generally, Islamic interpretations hold that the rights and responsibilities of a woman are equal to those of a man, but they are not necessarily identical. Men and women are created equal but not identical.

In traditional Islamic societies of the Middle East, women are not socially independent. They need men to act on their behalf, especially in the public domain. They are often secluded from males in education and from male visitors in the home. They ask permission to leave the house. They are limited in work opportunities outside the home.

The veiling of Islamic women, thus, is more than a cloth covering around their bodies. Veiling is symbolic of a way of life in which women are distinct from men. Veiling is often seen in the seclusion, segregation, and separation of women from men and in women from public life.

WOMEN AND MEN IN HEAVEN AND HELL

Men and women appear to have different roles in the hereafter than those they have had on earth. A tradition relates that, at the coming judgment day, women will increase in number and men will decrease so that fifty women will be looked after by one man. Paradise will be a place of beauty as well as a place of sensual and sexual delights. It will be populated with delightful maidens, sometimes called houris. These maidens appear to be virgins whom no man or spirit has previously touched. These are favors of God. (Quran 55:54–56; 44:54)

Both the Quran and the traditions refer to weddings in heaven. In one tradition wives are kept in separate quarters from each other and from the men. Husbands may discreetly visit them.

Hell is described as a place of fire, boiling water, a roasting place full of pus. One tradition reports Muhammad as saying that he stood at the gates of hell and found that the majority of people entering were women. Another tradition relates that Muhammad said a woman entered hellfire because of a cat she had tied, neither giving it food nor setting it free to eat from the earth. In these two traditions, inferences are made that more women go to hell than men and that a cat may be more worthy than a woman.

A BABY IS BORN

Family is very important in Islam. Children are a sign of God's blessing, and often more children mean more blessings. There is much happiness in anticipation of the birth, during the birth, and in the days afterward.

The baby is given a name, and a Muslim religious leader is present to speak the blessings of God. It is most appropriate to give gifts at the time of the baby's birth and to visit and show pleasure and to wish God's good favor upon the family.

SAYING HELLO

The traditional greeting is *"Salam alekum,"* "Peace be on you." The response is *"We alekum salam,"* "And on you be peace." The Quran tells

Muhammad to greet others by saying, "Peace be upon you." This is also the greeting given to the blessed in paradise.

Muslims also shake hands. Men may embrace men in greeting. Men do not generally touch women. It is standard in greeting to inquire about the health of the person and family and to make polite conversation before engaging in serious matters.

EATING AROUND THE TABLE

Diet is important in keeping a pure heart, a sound mind, a healthy body, and a soul bound for eternity. Islam teaches that certain foods and drinks are prohibited. Forbidden foods include the flesh of swine, the meat of dead animals and birds, and anything slaughtered with the invocation of any other name than God. Drinks which are harmful to morality and the body are intoxicants, including alcoholic beverages and certain drugs.

The general principle is that all foods which are pure and good for humanity are allowed for eating in moderate amounts. One would not serve pork products to Muslims who are guests around the table. It is not discourteous to inquire of the likes and dislikes of guests concerning food when it is known they come from rather strict religious backgrounds.

The right hand is used for eating. The left hand is avoided because Muslims believe that Satan uses the left hand. Also it is taboo because of its use in relieving oneself.

CLOTHING

The principles of decency, modesty, and chastity govern Islamic dress. Arrogance and false pride must not be stimulated nor should morality be called into question or weakened.

Men are warned not to wear pure silk, gold, and certain precious stones, for these are better suited for women. Women are to wear clothing that exemplifies their dignity and chastity. They must not be the subjects of idle gossip or suspicions or rumors.

The Quran does stipulate that women should draw their veils over their bosoms and not display their beauty except to their husbands and close family members. Various styles of veils are worn by Muslim women across cultures. Some veils expose only eyes and nose while others flow freely across the shoulders. Certain orthodox Islamic governments tightly control the veiling of women, while other Muslim societies allow great latitude in women's dress.

Both men and women are to dress with respect to their natures and natural instincts given them by God. God condemns men who behave in a woman's fashion and women who behave in a man's fashion. However, harmless items of clothing are considered beautiful gifts of God.

Entertainment and Sports

Tradition reports that Muhammad encouraged sports and entertainment that strengthened morals and spiritual and physical well-being. Most Muslim forms of worship, including daily prayers with their *rakahs*, the fasting season, and the pilgrimage rituals use good exercise techniques and nurture the body.

Islam prohibits gambling because it subjects life to luck and mere chance. It is considered a frivolous and dangerous threat to mental and emotional stability and upsetting to normal patterns of life and work.

Alcoholic consumption is unlawful in Islam because it destroys health, depresses the mind, dulls the soul, absorbs wealth, destroys families, abuses human dignity, and violates morality. Islam bans alcohol drinking from both individual and community life.

The most popular form of entertainment and recreation among Muslims is family gatherings. Family and friends may gather around tables for meals in homes and on picnics. If visiting is not done regularly, it may be considered improper social behavior and insulting to the person who is not visited. A popular sport is football, known as soccer in the West. Muslim children learn early to kick a soccer ball in the yard or street.

Animals

A dog is considered unclean. It is a term of vilification against one's enemies, especially against unbelievers. A dog is only justifiable for herding, hunting, and protection. If a dog comes into contact with food or eating utensils or the surroundings of a mosque, the resulting impurity requires ritual purification. Satan is believed to appear in the form of a black dog.

The camel is an animal for transportation and brings other amenities to the owner. It is mentioned in the Quran as an example of God's wisdom and kindness. It may be sacrificed at special celebrations and festivals. A tradition reports that Muhammad looked with favor upon the cat as a pure animal, saw cattle as a gift of God, and appreciated horses.

Virtues and Vices

Muslims are to cultivate social virtues and to avoid social vices. Islam does not condone frivolous pleasures, lying, slander, arrogance, boasting, scheming, obscenity, insult, spite, envy, and inconstancy.

It encourages kindness, generosity, feeding the poor, visiting the sick, escorting the deceased to the grave, honoring the aged, and peaceful relations. A Muslim should be the first to give greetings and should restrain anger. One's word is to be one's bond.

THE WEDDING

Before a marriage, two things must occur. The man must arrange a dowry for the wife which is pleasing to her and her family. And the man and woman must sign a marriage contract. The signing is before an imam or judge with two Muslims present as witnesses.

After the signing of the marriage contract, the wedding may take place. The wedding is a public event celebrating the contract entered into by the couple. Marriage is not a sacrament in Islam; it is a social contract to establish a family unit. Family and invited guests attend the wedding with much festivity and gift-giving.

Traditionally, the couple consummate the marriage after the wedding. The virginity of the bride is established with a blood stain on a white cloth, signifying the breaking of the hymen.

THE FUNERAL

The confession (*shahada*) should be on the dying lips of a Muslim. After death, the body will be buried quickly, usually within twenty-four hours. Islam prohibits cremation because of its belief in the resurrection of the body.

The funeral rites include the washing of the body, the shrouding, the prayers, and the burial. The ablution of the body is carried out with several washings similar to purifications before prayers. A man washes a man, and a woman washes a woman.

Layers of cloth are used in shrouding the body. A veil is also included for the woman. The body is faced in the direction of Mecca as the imam recites prayers and reads al-Fatiha, the opening chapter of the Quran.

Mourners usually say prayers at the mosque for the dead and at other times. As the body is carried to the cemetery for burial, the confession is chanted. The body is buried with the right side facing Mecca. Burial is usually in traditional funeral wrapping rather than a coffin, though coffins are not prohibited. The funeral wrapping is a seamless white shroud and may have been dipped in the well of Zamzam near Mecca during the pilgrimage.

BACKGROUND ASSUMPTIONS IN MEETING MUSLIMS

Muslims come from many cultures, languages, and ethnicities. What unites them all is the Quran, the sayings and deeds of their prophet Muhammad, and the sharia law traditions. Muslims may bring different cultural and even religious understandings to relationships. Often there are differences between Sunnis and Shiites as well as between orthodox and folk Muslims.

The following may serve in general to present some assumptions which Muslims bring to conversations:

- Islam is the one true religion. It is inconceivable that anyone would want to be anything but a Muslim.
- When non-Muslims learn about Islam and realize that it is the one true way, they will convert.
- When one refers to leaders of Muslim countries and groups such as Saddam Hussein of Iraq or Arafat of the PLO as voices for Islam, one is reminded that one is only a true Muslim who follows the Quran and the sayings of the prophet Muhammad.
- Male family members have the right and the obligation to maintain family honor and to provide for and protect the women.
- All good things, including education, jobs, marriage, housing, and recreation, come through the family. The individual is an intricate part of the family. The family looks after its own and stays together.
- The woman's basic place is in the home. She fulfills part of her duties as a wife by bearing male offspring.
- One should offer a guest food and/or drink. One should not offer it with the left hand. It is used for cleansing oneself.
- To tell a guest no is impolite. One will do one's best to oblige a guest.
- It is a son's duty to take care of parents in their aging years.
- The Western powers practice imperialism against Islamic nations and Muslim peoples. The nation of Israel is illustrative of this practice.
- Christianity is a religion of polytheism, believing in three gods in its teachings of the Trinity.
- The future is in God's hands. It would be presumptuous for one to predict the future or even to assume there will be a future. *Enshallah,* if God wills.

CHAPTER 8

MUSLIMS AND SOME BIG ISSUES

TENSION BETWEEN TRADITION AND CHANGE

A great challenge for Muslims is the tension which often exists between tradition and change. Traditionalism primarily seeks its answers and expressions in what the Quran says, what the prophet Muhammad said and did, and the actions of the Muslim leaders during the formative days of Islam. Change in itself is not viewed as bad. However, it must be evaluated by the norms of Islam.

Halal and *haram* are two concepts which refer to right and wrong behavior. *Halal*, meaning "permitted," is that behavior which is pure and safe. *Haram*, meaning "prohibited," is action which is impure and harmful. For example, capital punishment is halal and homosexuality is haram.

Often challenges have come when Islam has left its original Arab culture and language and become a part of another culture and language. Also, its impact with the Western world and the influences of modernization often have been stressful and testing.

The following are some areas in which Islam has sought answers to tough issues in the modern world. Its answers not only affect the communities of Muslims but also relate to non-Muslim neighbors.

BIRTH CONTROL AND POPULATION

Islam is not an ascetic religion. It emphasizes family and community and encourages couples to have many children. The Quran has no specific statement about contraception and birth control. It does say that God bestows children and leaves barren whom he wills.

The primary method of contraception at the time of Muhammad was coitus interruptus. Traditions associated with Muhammad indicate that he was not opposed to this method of contraception. Muhammad counseled men to marry women who would give birth to many children which would result in great pride for the nation of Islam.

The respected jurist-scholar al Ghazali of the twelfth century wrote that coitus interruptus was permissible. He cited three reasons: protection of the wife from any risk related to childbirth, prevention of excessive hardship on the family, and undue financial burden.

Various Islamic nations have attempted to implement programs of family planning, often encouraged with grants from the United Nations. Pakistan did so and encountered opposition from the *ulama*. They opposed family planning because it:

- Resembled infanticide
- Was unnatural to human nature
- Demonstrated disbelief in the providence of God
- Ignored the prophet's admonition to increase in numbers
- Would lead to disastrous social consequences
- Was part of a conspiracy of Western imperialists against developing nations.[1]

Muslim authorities consider other forms of contraception. The douche, condom, diaphragm, and pill are undesirable but not unlawful to *sharia*. Vasectomy, tubal ligation, and hysterectomy are irreversible methods which are prohibited.

Biotechnological modern methods are being debated by the authorities. Artificial insemination may meet the higher goals of birthing a child. Sperm banks are condemned as an illegitimate act. In vitro fertilization must be restricted to a single ovum but is still questionable. Surrogate parentage is illegitimate.

The Islamic ideal is to have many children. Across Islamic cultures husbands and wives have resorted to many solutions to barrenness and infertility. They include polygamy, amulets, herbs, magic spells, and foster children. In summary the Quran has no explicit reference to birth control and contraception. Schools of jurists have ruled that birth control is undesirable and improper though not unlawful and prohibited.

ABORTION

Islam upholds the sanctity of life as God creates it. The Quran does not deal specifically with abortion. Abortion is the termination of a pregnancy before the natural period of gestation. It may be spontaneous or by intervention. Islam is concerned with abortion by human intervention.

In the Islamic view there are justifications for ending life. Highway robbers may be executed. In the Quran, adultery is dealt with by one hundred stripes; Muhammad added stoning. Apostasy for one who renunciates Islam may have fatal consequences. Murder demands a just retribution. Jihad or holy war results in killings.

However, with abortion Muslim jurists consider the status of the soul of a fetus. Tradition holds that after 120 days the fetus has a soul. Jurists generally agree that after the fetus is completely formed and has a soul, abortion is prohibited and even considered a crime.

Among jurists in general, abortion which results from illegitimate sex is not justified. Rape does not necessarily justify abortion, but violent rape might. A fetus which may be determined to be mentally deformed does not justify abortion. If a mother's health in pregnancy is determined to incur her death unless there is an abortion, then it may be appropriate.

Thus abortion, with few exceptions, is not allowable. A basic understanding which underlies any discussion of abortion is in the context of marriage and sex within that relationship. Every human being has a right to be born and to live as long as God permits. If abortion occurs except for the expectation of risk upon the mother's life, it amounts to murder according to Islam.

HOMOSEXUALITY

Islam condemns homosexuality. Islamic scholars point to the Quranic story of Lot and his family and community and the experience of sexual deviancy. God condemned the sexual deviant behavior in the time of Lot. The people of Lot are declared the first to originate homosexuality, and therefore Islam denies the natural tendency from birth.

It is declared offensive to society, corrupting in its lifestyle, and in violation of the Quran. It is linked to violence and aggression against others. Muslim theologians consider homosexuality a major sin, for Islam presents a high view of marriage and family. Sexual relations are to be experienced in the marriage relationship. The basic and primary goal of sex is for procreation within the limits of marriage. Thus, homosexuality is not only condemned by the Quran, but it also violates human nature and the standards of orderly society.

AIDS

AIDS is the acronym for Acquired Immunodeficiency Syndrome. Muslim writers acknowledge that it is a worldwide problem. It involves more than an individual illness. Its effects are physical, mental, and social.

Certain known factors which cause AIDS are illicit intravenous drug use, homosexuality, bisexuality, multiple sex partners or sexual relations with an infected person, babies born to mothers who are HIV positive, accidental punctures with needles contaminated with the virus, and transfusions with HIV, contaminated blood and blood products.

Islam teaches strong views on God's purposes in creation of law and order in individual and community life. The Quran teaches high standards and practices for health and hygiene, for sex within marriage, and for the purification and cleanliness of the body as well as the soul.

Prevention is the key concept in Islam with regard to AIDS. Muslims teach the absolute abstinence from illicit drug use and of sex outside of marriage.

Euthanasia and Suicide

God alone gives life and alone takes life. To take one's own life is to disobey God and to turn from the path of Islam. Death ends a person's opportunity to perform good deeds. It also carries one from one type of existence to another. Heaven and hell reflect what one's reward is from deeds in temporal life. Thus, hell is the destination for committing suicide.

The Quran admonishes not to kill oneself because God has been most merciful. Several traditions concerning Muhammad describe his views on suicide. Whoever kills himself with poison or throws himself from a mountaintop will end up in hellfire forever. Another tradition relates that a soldier grew impatient with his wound and used a knife to stab himself further. Muhammad forbade him to enter paradise.

Islam teaches that true believers know that hardships come from God and not from others. They must accept problems with patience and endurance. God is merciful to those who repent and seek righteousness.

Islamic jurisprudence determines that death is the complete departure of life or soul from the body. Physical death is the cessation of the pulse and the uninterrupted cessation of the heartbeat. Brain death cannot be considered a clear evidence of death. Life is as long as the heart beats. Thus, disconnecting life-support systems is not considered killing or cause of death. True life does not come from machines.

CAPITAL PUNISHMENT

The Quran asserts that a life which Allah has created should not be taken except in the way of justice. (6:152) The way of justice means following the law or sharia with a properly appointed Islamic judge making decisions and sentencing. The execution is carried out by the legitimate authorities.

Three crimes may merit the death penalty.

1. Unjust murder. The law of retaliation is put into effect in the judicial process.
2. Adultery with someone else's spouse. Four eyewitnesses are necessary for verification. Either a husband or wife can be charged with the crime.
3. Apostasy from Islam. One who embarrasses, ridicules, or blasphemes Islam may be subject to execution. Muslims who have chosen another religion have been put to death. In some Muslim countries, apostasy is sometimes associated with treason against the state.

INTERRELIGIOUS MARRIAGE

Interreligious marriage is permitted for the husband only. Children must be reared in the teachings of Islam and must be Muslims. If a Muslim woman marries a non-Muslim man, it is *haram*. If there are children, they must be raised as Muslims.

WEALTH AND EARNING INTEREST

While wealth is encouraged and favored by God, it is to be shared with the poor. The Quran states, "The Evil One threatens you with poverty and bids you to unseemly conduct. God presents you His forgiveness and bounty." (2:268) The collection of wealth will not bestow eternal life. (104:1–3)

Islam teaches that wealth should be earned. Thus gambling, cheating, and taking of interest is *haram*. Usury exploits people's need for money. In modern times the prohibition of loaning money without interest is a test on Islamic observance by financiers of Islamic governments and banking systems.

RELIGION AND STATE

The history and theology of Islam have found much trust and pride in the synthesis of religion and politics. Its worldview has been one of "we" versus "they." The world of Islam is always over against the world of ignorance or warfare against Islam. Thus, Islam appears to be a promoter of theocracy, that is, rule in the name and law of God.

Early Islam took the form of a theocracy. Muhammad, following visions from God, ruled in God's name. What became known as "The Constitution of Medina" was the blueprint for the community of believers and their relationships with nonbelievers.

The constitution gave Muhammad the power and authority not only to be prophet (which he already had from the revelations from God) but also political leader, judge, worship leader, and commander in chief. He could pay blood money and ransom captives. He made peace or declared war with enemies.

All disputes were handled by Muhammad, and he gave out justice. He received one-fifth of all the spoils from war. After the Jews were defeated, they were given certain religious rights and brought under political leadership of the Muslim community.

Islam has had varieties of political expressions. The last great vestige of a monolithic Islamic political and legal system passed with the demise of the Ottoman Empire in the 1920s. The last half of the twentieth century saw a variety of political expressions within predominant Muslim countries. There have been Islamic republics. Some governments have meshed together Islamic and secular systems. Others have established secular regimes with lip service to Islamic values.

A gathering of worldwide Islamic leaders in London in 1980 issued a statement for the establishment of an Islamic Order. It cited that only God confers authority on rulers, governments, and institutions, and that an Islamic government must follow the mandatory principles in the Quran and in the traditions. The statement emphasized brotherhood, justice, and consensus. It did not mention individual liberty or political freedom.[2]

Many Muslims desire an Islamic state. However, its form and substance, as well as whether it is democratic or monarchical, is debated. The traditional view is that the state which is governed by Islamic law is *dar al Islam*, the nation of believers or peace.

If the Islamic state is subjugated politically or economically by a non-Muslim nation, it is living in the *dar al harb*, in the nation of unbelievers or war. The Muslim community has two choices. There may be jihad (struggle or war) to gain independence and reestablish the Islamic state, or there may be migration to another territory.

Muslim communities express themselves differently with regard to religion, state, and politics. Indonesia, a nation with a plurality of Muslims, governs upon a secular model with freedom of religion. Saudi Arabia faces tension between traditionalism and modernism in governing, but it is heavily influenced by Islamic law and also allows little expression of freedom of religion. Iran has attempted through its formation of an Islamic republic to govern by Islamic principles.

The ideal of governance for Muslims remains the teaching of the Quran and the traditions of the prophet Muhammad. Tensions are faced in Islam's encounter in modern politics, governance, and economics.

WAR AND PEACE

If one stereotype exists among non-Muslims about Islam, it is that it is a religion of hostility and war. The one word many know about Islam from the mass media is *jihad*. Jihad is known as "holy war." Muslim writers in turn claim that non-Muslims are misinformed about the nature and intent of Islam and that it is a religion of peace.

Muslim jurists have written of four types of jihad. It is a war waged by the heart, the tongue, the hand, and the sword. The war of the heart is the internal spiritual and moral struggle to please God. The war of the tongue is to speak the truth of Islam. The hand represents setting forth the good moral example for the community. The war of the sword is armed conflict with the enemies of the Islamic community.

The enemies of God are those who threaten the existence of the Islamic community and peace, who persecute Muslims, and the polytheists. The enemies of God are those who choose to live in the world or sphere of ignorance and disbelief separate from Islam.

The world or sphere of Islam must conquer and rule over those of ignorance and disobedience. It is the classical Islamic view of "we" and "they," *dar al Islam* versus *dar al harb*. The peace of the world cannot be secured until the peoples come under the rule and protection of Islam.

For force or jihad to be employed to extend the sphere of Islam and to achieve peace, traditional Sunni jurists have set forth the following rules:

- There must be a just cause (the refusal of a non-Islamic political entity to acknowledge the sovereignty of Islam).
- There must be a declaration of Muslim intentions (the Muslim ruler must invite the enemy to accept Islam or to pay tribute and accept his authority).
- There must be the rightful Muslim ruler with authority.
- The war must be waged according to the right path of Islam.[3]

Islam has in the past labeled Jews and Christians "People of the Book" and has given them special minority status under the rule of Islam. The payment of poll taxes was required. They were allowed to follow some of their personal and family laws. Their freedom of worship was restricted in that they were never to proselytize Muslims.

History demonstrates that wars have been fought between Muslims and Jews and Christians. It is well documented by Muslims themselves of the slaughter of tribes of Jews by the prophet Muhammad and his warriors.

Thus, Islam is a religion of war and peace. The Quran prescribes war in the name of God. It promotes the slaying of transgressors. It prohibits killings in the sacred mosque unless Islam's enemies initiate battle. At the same time Muslim scholars point out that Islam is a religion of peace. One of God's names is peace. The daily greeting of Muslims is peace.

FREEDOM OF RELIGION

With reference to freedom of religion, Islam refers to the Quran, which says there is to be no compulsion in religion. (2:256) In practicality this means if one is not born a Muslim, it is best to convert to Islam. If one does not convert to Islam, one may be tolerated with a minority status within the rule of Islam.

For Jews and Christians, minority status means certain freedoms of worship, of church organization, and of observance of religious customs associated with birth, marriage, family, and death. Christians, for example, may have their own sectarian law courts that may not conflict with the general law of Islam. It also means paying certain taxes as *dhimmis* or minorities for the protection of the Islamic authorities.

Islam has stringent rules on apostasy. The penalty for a Muslim converting to another religion varies from excommunication from family and community to death. Thus, a Muslim is not given the freedom of choice to leave Islam. Nor does Islamic rule give other religions freedom to evangelize among Muslims. Other religions may pay a severe penalty for proselytization.

The kingdom of Saudi Arabia, which is nearly 100 percent Muslim, prohibits public Christian meetings, building of churches, and missionary activity.

How, then, has Islam dealt with freedom of religion in the context of their claim to be a religion of the final truth of God? A three-pronged approach has existed when Islam has been a majority and the dominant political authority.

First, there is the Muslim majority who enjoy the full rights and privileges under sharia law.

Second, there are the Jews and Christians, known as *dhimmis* or "People of the Book." Because they are considered in special relationship to Islam, they are given special protection. They are afforded certain privileges of worship and community as well as formalities in administering some domestic family affairs of marriage, divorce, and inheritance. They must pay taxes to the authorities for services rendered.

W. Montgomery Watt has written concerning Muslim treatment of minorities: "On the whole Muslim colonist regimes behaved very fairly towards their minorities and did not oppress them. The worst that could happen was that in a time of crisis a mob could get out of hand and attack minorities, but this was rare. Apart from this, however, the members of the minorities always felt that they were second-class citizens, excluded from the Muslim elite and from many government positions. Moreover, while a Muslim man could marry a woman from the minorities, a man from the minorities could not marry a Muslim woman." In the status of protected minorities, Christians lived under Islamic colonialism, "but it was a relatively benign form of colonialism."[4]

A third group is called, for lack of a better word, "associates," or throughout Islamic history as the enemies of Islam. They were non-monotheists who rejected Islam and who refused to join a Jewish or Christian community. They have been treated in various ways according to the Islamic governments involved.

HUMAN RIGHTS

The Islamic perspective on human rights is based on the Quran, the traditions of the prophet Muhammad, and interpretations and rulings by jurists schooled in the Quran and the traditions. God grants human rights, and they are applicable to everyone. The Quran states that if rulers fail to judge by the light of God, they are no better off than unbelievers. (5:44)

Muslims are forbidden to be prejudiced against people of other races. They point to Muhammad's only wife other than Khadija by whom he had a child: she was a Copt from Egypt. Bilal, a black slave, was one of his first converts and the first person to chant the call to prayer. Islam does have a history of involvement in the slave trade in the Middle East and Africa.

Human rights in an Islamic state include the following general areas:

- The security of life and property, including non-Muslims.
- The protection of honor; one should not be defamed.
- The security of personal freedom; guilt must be proven in open court.

- The right to protest against tyranny.
- The freedom of association; formation of groups under certain rules.
- The freedom of conscience; there should be no compulsion in religion.
- The protection of religious sentiments.
- The protection from arbitrary imprisonment.
- The right to participate in the affairs or state; there should be consultation.

ISLAMIC FUNDAMENTALISM:
STRUGGLE BETWEEN NEW AND OLD

Fundamentalism is not an Arabic word. Western media use it to describe ultraconservative movements in Islam. It basically means Muslims look to the past for guidance. Specifically they believe the basics of the Quran, the sayings and actions (hadith) of the prophet Muhammad, and the experiences of the first three centuries of Muslims should serve as the guide for all later Islamic practices.

Islamic fundamentalism has incorporated to some extent the following concerns:

- The internal degeneration and outward decline of the Islamic religion.
- A return to the essentials of the teachings of the Quran, the hadith, and the sharia.
- A call for a jihad, a struggle and warfare, to rescue the Islamic community from decline and corruption and to establish its true and correct standing.
- A critique of and attack upon any forms of imperialism and colonialism advanced both by outside influences and tolerated by Islamic leaders themselves.
- A judgment against the moral decadence of Western values seen in the light of secularism and modernism compared to the straight path of Islam.
- An affirmation of the rights of Palestinians for a homeland, for the rights of Muslims to their holy sites in Jerusalem, and a condemnation of Zionism.

To see Islamic fundamentalism is to note the expressions of Islam in the Islamic Republic of Iran, the Wahhabi sect in Saudi Arabia, the Talaban of Afghanistan, and the extremists groups such as the Muslim Brotherhood, Islamic Jihad, and Hamas. It is to read the words of

Ayatollah Khomeini of Iran, al Wahhab of Saudi Arabia, and al Banna the founder of the Muslim Brotherhood in Egypt, and many others.

Khomeini desired his Islamic Republic to move beyond Iran to establish a global Islamic rule. Al Banna taught his Muslim Brotherhood that the Quran was their constitution to be forced upon Egypt. His later disciple, Qubt, said that Islam was the only genuine civilization and that it could not accept a situation which was half Islamic and half non-Islamic. These writers echo the thoughts and practices of many others in the Muslim world who urge true Islam and the subjugation of that other world.[5]

The world is divided into two separate areas: that of Islam with its absolute truth, purity, and correctness and that of the other world with its ignorance, disbelief, corruption, and disobedience. The other world is damned. It becomes the object of judgment, ridicule, and damnation. It also becomes the object of warfare to subdue it, to convert it, and to bring it under the domination of Islam.

One primary area of fundamentalism is to preserve the gender roles. Women become veiled, withdraw from the public domains, and assume home duties. They no longer need public education in the schools.

Sharia law becomes the norm of a truly Islamic community. There is a return to the schools of law of the early centuries of the advance of Islam. Western jurisprudence is discarded or selectively used.

Christianity is viewed as a corrupting and crusading religion. Its missionaries and agents must not be allowed entry. It must remain under suspicion and distrust. And where it exists among the indigenous peoples under the rule of Islam, it too must be subjugated.

Islamic fundamentalism is not only expressed in a more official way by leaders and their statements and programs, but it is also a mind-set among many Muslims. Most Muslims revere the Quran and hold the prophet Muhammad in high esteem and as exemplary. When ordinary decisions are to be made about personal and family matters, they turn to their roots, to the Quran, and to the teachings of their leaders. They desire to conserve their life in the Islamic way.

Many tensions and ambivalences occur when Muslim men and women travel abroad, especially to Europe and the United States, for education and travel. Many are trained to deal with the modern technologically based world. They return home to employ their training and skills and new ideas within their traditional framework of Islamic views and values and lifestyles.

Although there is an outcry against Western ideas and values, Muslims in the fundamentalist movement do not hesitate to employ Western products and practices of modernity. Governments in Muslim countries use

Western models of parliamentary and constitutional forms. Tanks, televisions, and T-shirts are bought and become symbols of prestige. Cokes and McDonald's hamburgers beckon Muslims to drink and eat.

Thus, within fundamentalism there is tension between the old ways and the new. Some Muslim leaders attempt to lead their peoples into secularism with trappings of Islam on the surface. Others choose what they believe is the best of the West and keep the best of Islam. Some decry the corruption and decay around them of both Islam and the West and advocate drastic action and change to bring forward true Islam. John Esposito, a contemporary scholar of Islam, has perceptively written:

> Islamic revivalism in its broadest sense refers to a renewal of Islam in Muslim personal and public life. Its manifestations include an increase in religious observances (mosque attendance, Ramadan fast, wearing traditional Islamic dress); a revitalization of Sufi (mystical) orders; proliferation of religious publications and media programming; calls for the implementation of Islamic law; creation of Islamic banks; and the growth of Islamic organizations and activist movements.

> Growing out of this context, Islamic revivalism has led to the reassertion of Islam in politics. Incumbent governments appeal to Islam for political legitimacy and popular support for policies and programs. Opposition movements use the language and symbols of Islam to criticize established governments, and to advocate actions ranging from sociopolitical reform to violent revolutionary action.[6]

CHAPTER 9

THE CLASH OF TWO GIANTS

Christianity and Islam

TWO MISSIONARY AND COMPETITIVE RELIGIONS

Christianity and Islam, both highly missionary and mobile religions, have faced each other for 1,400 years.

- At times they have ignored each other.
- Most of the time they have distrusted each other.
- Often they have diatribed against each other.
- Sometimes they have had open hostilities and fought each other with their armies.
- Occasionally they have promoted understanding and love toward one another.

There are over one and a half billion Christians. Muslims number over one billion. Numerically they together compose little less than half of the global population. They send their missionaries across the world to seek conversions and influence. Christianity and Islam, respectively, print their Bibles and Qurans in multiple languages. They train and send their missionaries to the far reaches of the globe. They build their churches and mosques and schools across cultures.

In the twentieth century Christianity saw the secularization of much of its base in Europe while Islam saw the same in the crumbling of the Ottoman Empire. Turkey and Iran, strong seedbeds of Islam, witnessed its demise under the Ataturk and the Shah. Africa became a continent of competition between Christian and Muslim missions. Some thirty million Muslims became visible across Europe, and North America saw an increase to over five million Muslims.

Islam made advances in Southeast Asia with significant numbers in Indonesia, Malaysia, and the Philippines. With the demise of the Soviet Union, Christian and Muslim missionaries rushed to the fledgling republics, including Russia, Uzbekestan, and Khazakstan.

Why are these two great world religions seen as competitors and foes of each other? Both profess monotheism, the belief in one God. They are religions based on revelation, prophets, and holy scripture. They offer their followers devotional, educational, and community experiences. They seem similar in many ways to an outsider.

But Christianity and Islam differ in essentials. What Islam denies about Christianity is what Christianity considers nonnegotiable. Islam believes the Bible has been corrupted by both Jews and Christians. It denies the divinity of Jesus, his crucifixion on the cross, and his death for the atonement of humanity's sin. On the other hand Christianity does not accept the Quran as the perfect word of God or that Muhammad is the final prophet.

Through the centuries Muslims have accused Christians of being polytheists, believing in more than one God. Christians have condemned the prophet Muhammad as the Antichrist. Muslims have lashed out against Western Christians for being imperialists and for sending their missionaries to convert Muslims to a corrupt religion. Christians have condemned Muslims for considering Muslim converts to Christianity as apostates and liable for death or excommunication.

Thus, the two giants throughout their histories have clashed more than they have conferred. Wars and rumors of wars between them have existed. The medieval Crusades have never been forgotten. Especially in the twentieth century Christians and Muslims have had open hostilities in Lebanon, Indonesia, Philippines, Sudan, Bosnia, and between Armenia and Azarbaijan. In the aftermath of the revolution which established the Islamic Republic of Iran, several prominent Iranian Christian clergymen disappeared or were killed.

Some scholars contend that Christianity and Islam will continue to clash along the lines of Islam versus the corrupted and corruptible Western Christianity. Some missiologists and church leaders see possibilities of conversations between the two on common concerns of justice and peace and certain social problems such as overpopulation and abortion.

Missionaries of both religions have different purposes and objectives. Muslims basically see their religion as a jihad against all nonbelievers and as the establishment of an Islamic world of institutions and values. Christians basically see their mission as one of reconciliation and peace in the name of Jesus Christ who was crucified on a cross for the forgiveness of sins of all people, including Muslims. The ultimate objective of Islam is to establish Islam. The ultimate purpose of Christianity is to proclaim the message of Jesus Christ.

MUHAMMAD, THE QURAN, AND CHRISTIANS

The prophet Muhammad had a primary purpose and plan once he had his visions and the solid, irrefutable word of God in the Quran. The plan was to establish Islam in the land. There were few Christians in Arabia. There were Jewish tribes. The Jews refused to convert or to graciously submit to his plan. He slaughtered some of them. Jewish wives and their children became wives and concubines of the Muslim warriors. Other Jewish tribes paid the taxes and obeyed Islamic laws.

The Arabs did not know much about Christians in Arabia. They had little accurate information about them. There was no Arabic translation of the Bible. Christianity throughout the Middle East had been in schism and controversy.

Muhammad, himself, knew only a smattering of the teachings of the Christians who had been declared heretics by the Church of Rome. Ibn Ishaq, a noted Arab historian, reported that Waraqa ibn-Nawfal, the cousin of Muhammad's wife Khadija, was a Christian and had some knowledge of the Christian Scriptures. Perhaps he knew some Scriptures in the Syriac language.

Muhammad had led trading caravans to Gaza, Damascus, and Christian Abyssinia, but little is known of any contacts with Christians. However, he knew enough to declare both Jews and Christians "People of the Book." This meant they had received perfect revelations in the original Torah and Gospel.

But according to Muhammad, these books had been corrupted. They needed the perfect revelation by the final prophet who brought the perfect Quran. Meanwhile, if Jews and Christians would not convert to Islam, they must submit to Islamic rulership while practicing their religions with restrictions.

Early passages in the Quran refer favorably to Christians. "Those who believe in the Quran, and those who follow the Jewish scriptures, and the Christians and the Sabians, any who believe in Allah and the Last Day, and work righteousness, shall have their reward with their Lord; on them shall be no fear, nor shall they grieve." (2:62)

As Muhammad established his community and invited the Jews and Christians to accept him as prophet, they refused. The later passages in the Quran report the results of the refusal: "The Jews say the Christians have naught to stand upon, And the Christians say the Jews have naught to stand upon. Yet they profess to study the same Book. But Allah will judge between them in their quarrel on the Day of Judgment." (2:113)

The Quran reported many things about Christian beliefs, speaking highly of the virgin Mary and the birth of Jesus. It also stated that Jesus was no more than a messenger and that Christians blaspheme who say that Allah is Christ the son.

"Allah will say, O Jesus the son of Mary, Didst thou say unto men, Worship me and my mother as god in derogation of Allah? He will say, Glory to Thee! Never could I say what I had no right to say." (5:116f, also 4:171; 5:72f) The Quran also stated that it appeared that Jesus died on the cross, thus denying the crucifixion.

Muhammad's mission was to win the Christians to his founding community. They refused. Thus, they were considered as "People of the Book" and given a limiting minority status in the emerging Islamic umma.

EARLY MUSLIM DISPUTES WITH CHRISTIANITY

After Muhammad's death in 632, Muslim forces marched across the Middle East, North Africa, and Spain, bringing Islam as the ruling force in religion and politics. Battles were fought with tribes, including Jews and Christians. Some converted. Others resisted. Many were brought into submission to Islam by living under the authority of Islam and the Empire.

Jews and Christians, for the most part, were allowed as "People of the Book" to administer their own personal laws of marriage, divorce, and inheritance. The millet system came into practice.

For example, Christian minorities were allowed to live in certain quarters of the city, build their own churches, and live their lives in some uniformity in the midst of the Muslim majority. They paid the poll tax. They gave allegiance to the Islamic ruler. They obeyed the laws. They did not proselyte Muslims. They were known as the *dhimmis*, the protected minority.

By 732 the Muslim advance into Europe from Spain was stopped when the Christian Charles Martel with his army defeated the Muslims at the Battle of Tours in France. Christians and Muslims had had a history of clashing. Muslims usually won. Christians usually assumed minority status. By this time Islam had advanced through Iran and India to the edges of China.

The medieval ages saw Islam rise to great heights in political organization, medical science, philosophy, architecture, literature, and

jurisprudence. Islamic civilization prospered. Some scholars characterized Christianity as living in the dark ages.

There were occasions of polemics and apologetics. Mansur Ibn
Sarjun, a Christian and the former controller of the Byzantine government, served the Muslim caliphate. His grandson, John, as a boy was the
playmate of Yazid, the caliph's son. John later became the bishop of
Damascus. He wrote a *Dialogue Between a Saracen and a Christian*, an
apologetic for eighth-century Christianity. His aim was to equip
Christians to understand Muslims whom he considered heretics and to
prepare them to face Muslims in apologetics.

Caliph Mahdi in 781 had conversations with Timothy, the head of
the Nestorian church in Iraq. He asked why Christians face the east
when they worship, why they worshiped the cross, and why they were
not circumcised. He accused Christians of believing that God married a
woman and had a son. He asked how Jesus could die if Jesus is God.
They were good questions. They arose out of Muslim misunderstandings
of the Christianity of the times.

THE CRUSADING SPIRIT: WARS OF WORDS AND DEEDS

Christian encounters with Muslims during the Middle Ages took
several shapes. There were wars. The Crusades were many, and the
deaths were great. There were polemics and apologetics by both
Christians and Muslims. And there were attempts at conversion of
Muslims by Christians.

The Land and Sea Battles

Prior to the crusading era (1095–1298), there was a revival of religious
feeling across Europe to establish more monasteries and to make more pilgrimages to shrines. The ultimate pilgrimage was to the Holy Sepulcher in
Jerusalem. Thirty years before the First Crusade of 1099, seven thousand
pilgrims traveled from the Rhine to Jerusalem. In 1076 a Muslim Turkish
emir who took control of Jerusalem under the authority of the Ottoman
Empire placed extreme difficulties upon Christian pilgrims.

In 1095, Pope Urban II called for a crusade to liberate Jerusalem and
the Holy Land from Muslims. Earlier, the Byzantine Christians had suffered a serious defeat by the Muslims in 1071 and had to withdraw from
Palestine and much of Asia Minor.

The Crusades occurred for various reasons: commercial rivalries
between Genoa and Venice, rivalries between the emerging nations of
Europe, the Pope's desire to reunite Christendom under his leadership,
and mounting resentment toward Muslims over their control of
Jerusalem and the Holy Land.

Armies assembled in Constantinople in 1097, marched south through Asia Minor, and captured Jerusalem from the Muslims in 1099. Four Crusader states were established: the kingdom of Jerusalem, principality of Antioch, and the countries of Edessa and Tripoli. Then, Muslims recaptured Edessa in 1144.

In 1187 the renowned Muslim general Saladin recaptured Jerusalem from the Christians. Saladin had become the master of Egypt and by 1174 was recognized as the sultan of the entire region from Mosul to Cairo. Saladin had engaged in jihad against the Christians in the area before the capture of Jerusalem. An event that had sparked his mission of jihad had been the sinking by a Christian vessel of a Muslim pilgrim ship on the way to Mecca in 1182.

There were many crusades during this era. Christian armies captured Acre and a part of the Palestinian coast in 1191 and held them for a hundred years. By the late eleventh century, however, strong Muslim leadership brought a virtual end to Christian control in the Holy Land.

Later Muslim writers saw the Crusades as a Christian jihad against Muslim lands and peoples. Some have viewed them as the beginning of European colonialism. Muslims through the centuries have used the Crusades as illustrations of the worst that is within Christianity.

The Wars of Words

The encounter with Islam during the Crusades deeply impressed Christians. Not much attention had been given Islam by Christianity. Polemics and apologetics became abundant. For the most part the Eastern Orthodox Christian theologians from the eighth through the thirteenth centuries castigated Islam as a heretical religion. Muhammad was called a false prophet and the Antichrist.

The poet Dante in *The Inferno* depicted a mutilated Muhammad languishing in the depths of hell. Thomas Aquinas wrote about Islam in his *Summa contra Gentiles*. His writings influenced the perceptions of Christianity toward Islam until well into the nineteenth century. Those perceptions were:

- Islam is a false and a deliberate perversion of truth.
- Islam is a religion that spreads by violence and the sword.
- Islam is a religion of self-indulgence.
- Muhammad is the Antichrist.

An Emerging Christian Approach

The encounter of Christianity with Islam also led Christians to gain more information about Muslims. As more knowledge was desired,

Christians also developed schools and programs of training to understand and reach out to the Islamic world. Thus, programs of missions were initiated. The theme of love was enunciated toward Muslims as well as their conversion to Christianity.

Peter the Venerable was the abbot of the monastery at Cluny from 1122 to 1156. He felt that the Crusades had omitted entirely the major Christian concern of the conversion of Muslims. Peter headed a monastic movement of 10,000 monks in 600 monasteries throughout western Christendom.

Peter set out to give European Christians an accurate account of Islam and to criticize the errors of Islam. He wrote concerning Muslims, "I attack you not as some do, by arms, but by words; not with force, but with reason, not with hatred, but in love . . . I love; loving, I write you; writing, I invite you to salvation."

He collected Latin works translated into Arabic, and under his influence the Quran was translated into Latin. He was criticized for his work toward Muslims by Bernard of Clairvaux. Peter responded that Islam was a Christian heresy and Christians needed to know Islam in order to respond to it.

His mission to Muslims in speaking and writing had influence later upon Martin Luther and Philip Melanchthon in 1543 when they wrote introductions to the publication of translations of the Quran and other Islamic writings.

Francis of Assisi (1181–1226) said that love rather than the crusading spirit should be demonstrated toward Muslims. He became a student of Islam. In 1219 he journeyed to Egypt and had the opportunity to preach to the Muslim Sultan. After hearing the Muslim call to prayer from the mosque minaret, he asked the monks to ring the church bells to announce worship services. His spirit of concern for love toward Muslims in the context of witnessing to them had influence upon later Christian missions.

Raymond Lull (1232–1316) is a pivotal figure in Christianity's relationship to the religion Islam and to Muslim peoples. He was born to a wealthy family on an island off the coast of Spain which had been regained from the Muslims at the time of his birth. He committed himself to a mission among the Saracens (Muslims) who were considered the most hated and feared enemies of Christians.

He wrote, "I see many knights going to the Holy Land beyond the seas and thinking that they can acquire it by force of arms, but in the end all are destroyed before they attain that which they think to have. Whence it seems to me that the conquest of the Holy Land ought . . .

to be attempted . . . by love and prayers, and the pouring out of tears and blood."

Lull's strategy to understand and reach out to Muslims was pursued through apologetics, education, and evangelism. He spent nine years in learning Arabic. He wrote some sixty books, many of which were devoted to Christianity and Islam. He established monasteries as training grounds with emphasis upon the Arabic language. At the Council of Vienna he persuaded leaders to have Arabic offered in European universities with the purpose to encourage understandings between Christians and Muslims.

Lull was a missionary to Muslims, traveling to Algeria and Tunisia and preaching to and holding meetings with Muslims. Several times he was persecuted and banished. In 1315, when he was eighty years old, Lull met his martyrdom in Algeria after preaching to and debating with Muslims. They stoned him to death.

Raymond Lull combined both a spirit of love toward Muslims and a strong polemic toward their beliefs and practices. Perhaps his fanaticism and theirs met to end his long life. His emphasis upon education, languages, and evangelism has been a model for other Christian generations to follow.

THE LAST FOUR HUNDRED YEARS: A RELATIONSHIP OF UPS AND DOWNS

About the time the Ottoman Empire began, Martin Luther launched the Reformation in 1517. His writings included little about Muslims. But what he wrote was scathing and portrayed hostility toward Islam. He characterized the Quran as a foul and shameful book. He described the Muslim Turks as devils following their devil god.

Luther wrote that Muhammad

> greatly praises Christ and Mary as being the only ones without sin, and yet he believes nothing more of Christ than that He is a holy prophet, like Jeremiah or Jonah, and denies that He is God's Son and true God . . . On the other hand, Mohammed highly exalts and praises himself and boasts that he has talked with God and the angels . . . From this anyone can easily see that Mohammed is a destroyer of our Lord Christ and His kingdom . . . Father, Son, Holy Ghost, baptism, the sacrament, gospel, faith, and all Christian doctrine are gone, and instead of Christ only Mohammed and his doctrine of works and especially of the sword is left.[1]

Although Christianity basically ignored Islam or disputed with it at a distance for the last four hundred years, there have been attempts at understanding its backgrounds, beliefs, and practices. The nineteenth century witnessed Christian attempts at translations of the Quran as well as missions toward Muslims. The twentieth century saw individual efforts by such as Samuel Zwemer to spend years among Muslim populations in education and evangelism. During the latter half of the twentieth century much effort was placed upon understanding the Muslim world as well as church mission agencies sending missionaries to areas of the greatest concentration of Muslim people groups.

Christians Considered Colonialists

By 1700 the Muslim Ottoman Empire was declining. European colonialism impacted Muslim territories across North Africa and the heartland of the Middle East. Missionaries from Europe came along with the political and commercial interests of their nations. France occupied Algeria and controlled Tunisia by 1830. Italy gained Libya by 1912. France had mandates over Syria and Lebanon, and Great Britain looked after Jordan and Palestine after World War II.

Islam felt a major intrusion with the signing of the Balfour Declaration in 1917 in which Britain guaranteed the Jews a national homeland in Palestine. The nation of Israel was formed in 1948. Muslims lost their authority over Jerusalem.

As Christian missionaries entered Muslim territories along with diplomats and business peoples, they were often considered colonialists by Muslims.

Henry Martyn (1781–1812)

Henry Martyn came to India under the umbrella of a business company. He entered India from England in 1806 as a chaplain with the East India Company. Martyn became one of the greatest Bible translators in Central Asia.

Upon his arrival he met William Carey, who encouraged him in translation work. His primary responsibility was as chaplain to the families of the employees of the East India Company.

Although he had fragile health, he spent four years at military posts establishing schools and preaching to both Indians and Europeans. He also translated the New Testament into Hindustani, Persian, and Arabic. In 1810 he traveled to Persia (Iran) to revise his Persian and Arabic translations. Martyn was a pioneer in missions to Muslims, especially in his translation work. He died in Asia Minor in 1812 at the age of thirty-one.

When he first arrived in India, he had written in his diary that he was ready to burn out for God. He did so in six years.

Debates and Exchanges

As the twentieth century approached, Muslims knew the basic perceptions of Christians toward them. The Religious Tract Society of London in 1887 published a pamphlet "The Rise and Decline of Islam." It described the falsehoods of its teachings, its spread by violence and the sword, its sexual indulgences, and the unseemly character of Muhammad.

Debates were held between Christians and Muslims. Carl Pfander, a German missionary, publicly debated Muslims in Iran and India. In his book *Balance of Truth*, translated into Urdu, he wrote of the superiority of Christianity over Islam. By 1852 the Muslim scholar Rahmat Kairanawi in his book *Revelation of Truth* attempted to refute Pfander. He debated Christian teachings, employing the new European biblical critical methods to condemn the missionaries' message. He emphasized how the Quran superseded the Bible and the false teachings of the trinity.

The Gospel of Barnabas: A Forgery

The Gospel of Barnabas is a work of over two hundred chapters and four hundred pages. It has been used by Muslims as an apologetic tool to illustrate the falsehood and inaccuracy of Christianity and to uplift their own prophet Muhammad.

The original manuscript is in Italian and came to light in Amsterdam in 1709. It was published by Christian scholars in English in 1907. Muslims published an Arabic translation in 1908 in Cairo, and other translations followed in Urdu, Persian, and dialects in Indonesia.

Much of the materials in the New Testament are included. However, there are many additions. It quotes lines from the Quran as well as from Dante's *Divine Comedy*. It was a Muslim tool for proving the superiority of Islam over Christianity. Two major emphases in *The Gospel of Barnabas* are that Jesus Himself denied that he was the Messiah and that Jesus Himself prophesied the future coming of the prophet Muhammad.

Christian scholars have suggested that *The Gospel of Barnabas* was written between the fourteenth and sixteenth centuries perhaps by a Christian convert to Islam. The author makes mistakes about Islam as well as about other matters, including placing Nazareth on the Sea of Galilee. Muslims utilize it to portray Jesus as the Isa of the Quran. Christians refute it as a forgery and as propaganda for Islam.

Attempts at Serious Understandings and Renewed Missions

Missionaries began to take seriously the religion Islam, the people called Muslims, and the cultural environment. Languages were learned, and the Bible was translated in languages of Muslim peoples. Customs were observed, including the time and energy involved in prayer five times a day and in the month of fasting. A missionary would serve no pork, which Islam had ruled was unclean, to a Muslim guest.

Orientalists became more familiar with Muslim scripture and tradition through their study of Islamic sources and the Arabic language. They criticized the historicity and authenticity of the traditions of the prophet Muhammad. Muslims viewed these criticisms as an attack on their religion. The Muslim scholar Ameer Ali wrote *The Spirit of Islam* to counteract the Orientalists.

Samuel Zwemer

In the early 1900s Samuel Zwemer, called the Apostle to Islam, focused the church's attention on Islam. He served as a missionary to Arabia, Bahrain, and Egypt. In the early years he established the American Arabian Mission. He and his wife pioneered missions to Muslims in most difficult circumstances, losing their four- and seven-year-old daughters to illness within eight days of each other.

In 1912 he moved to Cairo to serve the United Presbyterian Mission where he found a more open Muslim public. He made important contacts with the renowned university al-Azhar. He spoke to crowds sometimes totaling over two thousand Muslims. From his conservative theology he preached Christ while showing the utmost respect for Muslims.

For seventeen years, he traveled from Cairo to India, China, Indonesia, and South Africa, speaking, raising funds, and establishing work among Muslims. In 1929 he joined the faculty of Princeton Theological Seminary. For over forty years he served as editor of the journal *The Muslim World*. He wrote over fifty books and hundreds of tracts. His legacy has continued also in the Samuel Zwemer Institute of Muslim Studies in California. He made a great impact upon informing Christians about the need of evangelism among the Islamic peoples.

Zwemer has been the inspiration for both Christians and Muslims to seek to know each other's religions as well as to express the deepest levels of their faith to one another.

From Kenneth Cragg to Mahmoud Ayoub

Kenneth Cragg, an Anglican bishop and missionary in the Middle East, wrote a seminal book, *The Call of the Minaret*. It has received a wide reading from both Christians and Muslims.

Several Muslim writers, themselves, made overtures to the Christian community. Kamel Hussein, an Egyptian, wrote a novel, *City of Wrong*, which focused on the events in Jerusalem before and after the crucifixion of Jesus. Although he did not deal with the controversial question of whether Jesus actually died on the cross, he did write about the collective sin of Jesus' rejection on Good Friday.

Another writer, Mahmoud Ayoub, a Lebanese Shiite Muslim, wrote *Redemptive Suffering in Islam*. He wrote about the sufferings of Christ. He pointed to Jesus in the Quran as one of the servants of God and as the word of God. For him the Jesus of the Quran and of later Muslim piety is much more than a mere human being or the messenger of a book.

WARS AND RUMORS OF WARS INTO THE TWENTY-FIRST CENTURY

In 1,400 years of the coexistence of Christianity and Islam, there has been more hostility and suspicion between the two than friendliness and trust. There have been less St.-Francis-of-Assisi types among Christians and more *Gospel-of-Barnabas* types among Muslims. Nations against nations, tribes against tribes, families against families, and individuals against individuals.

Muslim militias have fought Christian militias in Lebanon. They have battled over land, over politics, over rulership of the country, and over long-standing family hostilities. Also, from time to time Muslims have fought other Muslims, and Christians have fought other Christians.

Indonesia has seen aggravation of tensions between Muslim communities and Christian communities. In times of national stress, animosities have emerged between the two, which have resulted in churches and mosques being burned and lives taken.

Conflicts are deep between the Christians in the south and the Muslims in the north of Sudan. The Muslim-dominated government has initiated Islamic reforms that have restricted the rights and freedoms of Christians. Wars have ensued. Tens of thousand of deaths have occurred. Some Christians have suffered crucifixions on crosses.

The Philippines, islands with a majority of Christians, has had religious divisions. Muslim insurgents have fought the government for land and political power. In eastern Europe, with the fall of communism, old religious wounds between Christians and Muslims emerged. Bosnia became a seedbed of war between the two. Instability has existed across other countries in the region because of religious and political tensions.

There has been animosity for decades between the Christians in Armenia and the Muslims in Azarbaijan, and battles have been fought. The establishment of the Islamic Republic of Iran under Ayatollah Khomeini brought strained relations with the minority Christian communities. All international Christian missionaries were asked to leave. Several prominent Christian pastors were slain amid mysterious circumstances. No one was apprehended.

There have been hijackings of planes and ships, terrorist bombings of airports, buildings, city centers, and buses in the name of Islam and in the name of Allah Akbar (God is Great). Lives have been lost.

Islamic jihad has not only been a threat against Christians but has remained a puzzle among Christians. If jihad has a personal meaning to struggle to please God by obeying commands and practicing rituals, then Christians may understand the life of a Muslim. But if jihad has a community meaning to go to war against infidels, polytheists, and those who oppose the way of Islam, then Christians may understand that they are subject to threats and subjugation and loss of freedoms in a minority status.

A deep seriousness in both Christianity and Islam accounts for a discomfort between them. The orthodoxy of Islam views Christianity as a corrupt religion. Its book is corrupt. Its teachings about the prophet Jesus are heretical. And its view of God is *shirk*.

On the other hand, the orthodoxy of Christianity sees Islam as a heretical and false religion. It understands that Islam denies the bedrock upon which Christianity is founded: that Jesus Christ is the Messiah, the divine Son of God who was crucified on a cross on behalf of the sins of all humanity and that there is salvation in no other than the crucified and risen Jesus Christ.

Both Christianity and Islam are missionary to their very core. Islam has a plan for the institutionalization of its religion for humanity. There is unity in the major beliefs. There is uniformity in the practices. And there is universalism in its implementation. Islam is the superior religion, and all others must submit.

Christianity presents a Person, Jesus Christ, with a message of confession, repentance, and forgiveness in the name and saving grace of Jesus Christ, and with participation in the fellowship of the church. There is freedom of religion and separation of church and state.

A basic question is: Can two religions with high-intensity missions coexist? Can they allow each other space not only to exist but to grow? Can they allow freedom for others to choose one or the other? Can they live in peace and not in war?

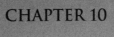

ISLAM'S VIEW OF
JESUS AND CHRISTIANS

MAJOR AFFIRMATIONS AND DENIALS

In the Christian world, the major message of Islam about Jesus is its denials of the basic beliefs of Christians. Questions arise in the Christian world: What has Islam got against Christianity? Why has Islam denied the great faith beliefs of Christianity which Christians believe are centered in the Bible and which have been taught by the orthodox church for some two thousand years?

In the Muslim world, the major message which Islam delivers about Jesus is the affirmations of the reverent titles given to him and the clarifications about the role of Jesus as a prophet. Within these affirmations are the underlying denials of the divinity of Jesus with all of its theological implications.

WHAT DOES ISLAM LIKE ABOUT CHRISTIANITY?

Islam has positive things to say about Christian matters. These positive views come directly from the Quran and the hadith. Sometimes they substantiate the sayings in the Bible. At other times they add additional favorable views, especially about Jesus.[1] They include the following:

- 🕮 The virgin Mary gives birth to Jesus (Isa).
- 🕮 Jesus is referred to with many titles, including prophet, messiah, word and spirit and mercy of God.
- 🕮 The Gospel (Injil) is positively referred to in the Quran.
- 🕮 There are positive references to Christians in the Quran.
- 🕮 Tradition reports that Jesus has a role in the events surrounding the end of the world and the judgment.

THE TITLES OF JESUS

The name given to Jesus in the Quran is Isa. Scholars believe that Isa came from the Syriac Yeshu, which was derived from the Hebrew Yeshua. The Christian form of the name Jesus comes from the Greek, which was a translation of the Hebrew Yeshua (Joshua). The meaning of the name for Christians is "God's salvation" or "he whose salvation is Yahweh." Isa is used in the Quran without explanation of its derivation.

The name Isa by itself occurs twenty-five times in the Quran. Altogether Isa is mentioned, along with other titles, in ninety-three different verses in some fifteen chapters. Jesus is given more honorific titles than any of the other prophets, including Muhammad.

As with the mention of any prophet, Muslims, when referring to the name of Isa, will say immediately, "Isa, on whom be peace." This practice, sometimes shown in print as PBUH (Praise Be Upon Him), may have been derived from a saying of Jesus, "Peace is upon me the day of my birth, and the day of my death, and the day of my being raised up alive." (Quran 19:33–34)

Son of Mary (Ibn Maryam)

The title "Son of Mary" occurs twenty-three times in the Quran. It is sixteen times as Jesus, Son of Mary, and seven times alone or with some other title. Son of Mary occurs only once in the Bible (Mark 6:3). There is no mention of Joseph in the Quran.

The Quran gives an account of the virgin birth of Jesus in Sura (chapter) 3. Mary is described as a virgin, chosen by God, and given much honor. Sura 3:42 reads, "Behold the angels said, O Mary! Allah has chosen thee and purified thee, chosen thee above the women of all nations."

Sura 34:45 continues, "Behold! the angels said, O Mary! Allah giveth thee glad tidings of a Word from Him: his name will be Christ Jesus the Son of Mary." Sura 3:47 relates, "She said, O my Lord, How shall I have a son when no man hath touched me? He said, Even so:

Allah createth what He willeth. When he hath decreed a Plan, He but saith to it, Be! and it is!"

Thus, the Quran affirms the virgin birth, and Muslims believe that Jesus was born of the virgin Mary. The birth is seen as a sign (*aya*) of God's power and as a miraculous event. Mary is given high regard. However, Jesus is presented as the son of Mary and not as the Son of God. For the Muslim it would be blasphemy (*shirk*) to associate the divine nature of Allah with human nature. In Sura 3, Jesus is compared to Adam by stating that both were created by Allah and were without a father.

The Messiah (Al Masih)

The title "messiah" is given to Jesus eleven times in the Quran. It is applied to periods of his life from birth to exaltation. Although no explanation is given for the title, the most likely meaning is from the Hebrew meaning "the anointed one." Sura 3:45 states with reference to the annunciation of the birth of Jesus, "His name shall be the Messiah, Jesus, son of Mary." The use of *messiah* is as a personal name, like *Jesus*.

The Quran warns the "People of the Book" not to consider Jesus other than a messenger from God. "O People of the Book, do not go beyond bounds in your religion, and do not say about God anything but the truth. The Messiah, Jesus, son of Mary, is only the messenger of God." (4:171) "The Messiah, son of Mary, is nothing but a messenger, before whose time the messengers have passed away." (5:75)

In the Quran the title of "messiah" is used as an equipping and commissioning task for Jesus of being prophet and messenger. The fuller role of Messiah being the Savior and bringer of salvation is found in the Christian Gospels and not in Quranic statements.

Prophet (Nabi) and Messenger (Rasul)

Jesus is called "prophet" once in the Quran and is referred to as "messenger" or "apostle" ten times. The distinction between prophet and messenger in the Quran appears to be as follows: every people has a messenger sent to them by God, but prophets are in the succession of Abraham and Adam, that is, the Hebrew, Christian, and Muslim prophetic tradition.

The prophet (*nabi*) in the Quran appears as a messenger who brings the revelation from God which becomes a book, namely, the Torah, the Zabur (Psalms), the Injil (Gospel), and the Quran. Thus, the prophets come to the "People of the Book." Jesus spoke from the cradle, "I am indeed a servant of Allah. He hath given me Revelation and made me a prophet." (Quran 19:30)

Jesus is named in the company of several prophets, including Abraham, Noah, and Moses. Sura 6:84f lists eighteen Hebrew prophets, including Jesus, and states, "These are they upon whom we have bestowed the Book, and the jurisdiction and the prophetic office." Sura 57:26–27 reads, "And We sent Noah and Abraham, and established in their line Prophethood and Revelation . . . . Then, in their wake, We followed them up with Our messengers: We sent after them Jesus, the son of Mary, and bestowed on him the Gospel."

There are twenty-eight prophets named in the Quran. Six were given special titles:

- Adam the Chosen of God
- Noah the Prophet of God
- Abraham the Friend of God
- Moses the Converser with God
- Jesus the Spirit of God
- Muhammad the Apostle of God.

Muhammad was also called the last and seal, the end of prophets. In the Bible Jesus was called a prophet (Mark 6:15; 8:28). Jesus also accepted the title (Mark 6:4; Luke 13:33). However, the Bible clearly teaches that both others and Jesus thought of himself as more than a prophet.

According to the Quran, every community has a messenger. (Quran 10:47–48) Thus, recognition is given to other religions as part of a general revelation from God. This is distinct from the special revelation given by prophets. Jesus stands in succession to other messengers. He ate food as they did and died as they did. (Quran 5:75, 79; 19:33–34)

Some messengers are given preeminence over others because of a particular divine task. Jesus is both prophet and messenger to whom "We gave preeminence over others." (Quran 2:253–254) Jesus had both Gospel and "evidences," meaning miracles. He was also supported and confirmed by the Holy Spirit.

A messenger in the Bible may be a human messenger. More often it is a heavenly messenger like an angel who brings good tidings. In Islam the title "messenger" is given to Muhammad, especially in the confession (*shahada*) which is voiced daily by praying Muslims, "Muhammad is the messenger or apostle (*rasul*) of God." In contrast, Jesus is particularly called the Messiah.

Word (Kalima) and Spirit (Ruh) of God

Two of the most enigmatic titles assigned to Jesus in the Quran are the Word of God and the Spirit of God. No other prophets, including Muhammad, are called such. Sura 4:171 asserts Jesus both as word and spirit: "Christ Jesus the son of Mary was no more than a messenger of Allah, and His Word, which He bestowed on Mary, and a Spirit proceeding from Him."

- John the Baptist is portrayed as confirming in Jesus the word of God: "Allah doth give thee glad tidings of Yahya (John) witnessing the truth of a Word from Allah, and besides noble, chaste, and a Prophet." (Quran 3:39)

And the angels said to Mary, "O Mary, Allah giveth thee glad tidings of a Word from Him: his name will be Christ Jesus. The son of Mary, held in honour in this world and the Hereafter and of the company of those nearest to Allah." (Quran 3:45)

Muslims explain Jesus as "word" in terms of being a prophecy or of coming with a word, as messenger. In the Bible the Word (*logos*) is one of the most significant titles given to Jesus as seen in the Gospel of John and the First Epistle of John. In Islam there is no connection, as in Christianity, of Jesus as Word with Jesus as Son of God or with the incarnation of Jesus being the Word who becomes flesh.

The use of the word *Spirit* is connected to Jesus seven times in the Quran. He is confirmed or supported by the Spirit of Holiness or the Holy Spirit. (Quran 2:87, 253; 5:110) At other times God breathes His Spirit into Mary as she conceived Jesus. (Quran 4:171; 19:17; 21:91; 66:12) Not only at his birth but while Jesus was in the cradle and as a youth and adult, the Quran reports that He was supported by the Holy Spirit.

Later Muslim authors have written of Jesus as the Spirit and the Spirit of God. Tradition reports that Muhammad said that Jesus the son of Mary was the spirit of God and His Word which he cast to Mary the virgin.

The title Spirit was not emphatically applied to Jesus in the Bible. Spirit or *pneuma* is used in the Bible as "wind," "breath," "a spirit," and "the Holy Spirit." The Holy Spirit as divine presence and power descended upon Jesus at His baptism. In Romans 8:9, the Spirit of God and the Spirit of Christ are closely associated. It is in the understanding of the Trinity that Father, Son, and Spirit are joined together. Islam denies the Trinity.

Other Titles of Jesus

- **Servant (*abd*),** especially Servant of God
- **Sign (*aya*),** a sign from God and a sign to the people
- **Parable or Example (*mathal*),** appointed to be a parable
- **Witness (*shahid*),** a witness at the judgment
- **Mercy (*rahma*),** a mercy from God

- **Eminent (*wajih*),** an eminent one in this world
- **One Brought Near (*min al muqarrabin*),** one brought near to God
- **One of the Upright (*min al salihin*),** one of the righteous
- **Blessed (*mubarak*),** blessed wherever He is

THE MIRACLES OF JESUS

The miracles of Jesus are described in two major references in the Quran in broad strokes with little detail or comment. (3:49 and 5:110)

Sura 5:110 states,

> Then will Allah say: "O Jesus the son of Mary! Recount My favour to thee and to thy mother. Behold! I strengthened thee with the holy spirit, so that thou didst speak to the people in childhood and in maturity. Behold! I taught thee the Book and Wisdom, the Law and the Gospel. And behold! thou makest out of clay, as it were, the figure of a bird, by My leave, and thou breathest into it, and it becometh a bird by My leave, and thou healest those born blind, and the lepers, by My leave. And behold! thou bringeth forth the dead by My leave. And behold! I did restrain the Children of Israel from violence to thee when thou didst show them the Clear Signs, and the unbelievers among them said, 'This is nothing but evident magic.'"

The Quran indicates that Jesus healed the blind and the lepers and raised the dead to life. It also reports that Jesus made birds from clay. Except for reporting these miracles, there is little else said. Muslim writers have inferred that these miracles were done with the permission of God to convince the people of Jesus' mission. They were signs of his prophecy. It is to be noted that Muhammad did not attribute any miracles to himself.

The Bible gives various incidents of Jesus' healing the sick. Jesus raises the dead in the cases of the daughter of Jairus, the widow's son at Nain, and Lazarus (Mark 5:21–43; Luke 7:11–15; John 11). The Bible gives the details of the miracles and attributes them to Jesus' compassion for the needy. The Quran speaks of the "evidences" of Jesus. They are his teachings as well as his miracles in the prophetic tradition.

THE GOSPEL (*INJIL*) IN THE QURAN

Since its inception, Islam has affirmed the sacred tradition of the scriptures of Judaism and Christianity, as well as its own. Sura 3:3–4 is addressed to Muhammad: "He hath sent down to thee the Book with the truth, confirming what was before it, and he sent down the Torah and the Gospel aforetime as guidance for the people, and he sent down the Furqan." The Furqan is revelation.

Besides the Torah and the Gospel, the Quran mentions the Zabur, which is the book of David, the Psalms, and the Hikma, the Wisdom, which is given to prophets but in no particular book.

The word *injil* refers to Christian revelation which is associated with Jesus. Its origins come from the Greek meaning "evangel," "good news," or "Gospel." An ongoing question is whether Islam considers the *injil* or Gospel as mentioned in the Quran as restricted to what Jesus preached or to the entire New Testament.

Injil occurs twelve times in the Quran. Sura 57:27 asserts, "We gave Jesus the Gospel." It is to be noted that foundational to the sacred books of Torah, Gospel, and Quran is the archetypical "Mother of the Book" which is in heaven. (Quran: 43:3–4; 13:39; 3:7) The messengers or prophets receive from God their revelations or books whose original copy is in heaven.

Considerable discussion has ensued over the years among Muslim scholars concerning whether the *injil* of the Quran is the same as the Gospels in the Bible. A general view has held that the *injil* of Jesus was perfect and that the later Gospels, if not in their nature then in the interpretations of them, became corrupt and contaminated.

The Quran has asked all "People of the Book" to follow their scriptures or "Books." God gave Jesus the Gospel. It contains guidance and light and confirms the Torah before it. Likewise, the revelation to Muhammad and to Muslims came in the Quran: "To thee We sent the Scripture in truth, confirming the Scripture that came before it, and guarding it in safety." (5:48)

THE "PEOPLE OF THE BOOK" IN THE QURAN CALLED CHRISTIANS (*NASARA*)

Christians are called "Nasara" in the Quran. The name probably came from Syriac and may have originated from the word *Nazarene*. It is used fifteen times, fourteen of which are in association with the Jews. Christians and Jews are also referred to as "People of the Book." In recent times Christians have been called "Isawi" or "Masihi," followers of Jesus or Christ.

Christians are praised in some parts of the Quran. Their differences with the Jews and Muslims are pointed out. Their exclusiveness is decried. Their sectarian differences are criticized. Christian monasticism is questioned regarding its corruption.

At times Christians are warned about their beliefs in associating Jesus with God in their teachings on the Trinity and Son of God. Sura 3:64 reads, "Say O People of the Book! come to common terms as between us and you: That we worship none but Allah; that we associate no partners with Him; that we erect not from among ourselves Lords and patrons other than Allah."

The Quran counsels Muslims and Christians not to dispute but to believe in the one God. "Dispute not with the People of the Book save in the fairer manner and say . . . We believe in what has been sent down to us, and in what has been sent down to you; our God and your God is One." (29:46)

Seldom were Christians and Muslims reconciled in their differences. Thus, the Quran indicates that God tries them and will eventually resolve their difficulties. They are to excel in good works. "Had God so willed, he would have made you one community, but He hath not done so in order that he might try you in regard to what has come to you; so strive to be foremost in what is good; it is to God that ye return, all of you, and he will announce to you that in which ye have been differing." (5:48)

MUSLIM TRADITIONS ABOUT JESUS

The Quran has little to report about Jesus after his "appearance" at the crucifixion. Muslim traditions, however, have various stories of his latter days, and Muslims through the ages have reverenced Jesus in many ways with prayers and saints' tombs.

Some traditions associate Jesus with the *Mahdi,* the one who will return in the end times. Jesus will come from heaven, battle the Antichrist, and defeat him. Jesus will confess Islam, break all crosses, kill all swine, and usher in a millennium of peace and righteousness. There is a tradition that he will marry and have children. Both Jesus and Muhammad are given prominent roles at the great judgment day and at the time of God's issuing of rewards for heaven and hell.

There are shrines and saints' tombs named after Jesus (Isa) scattered across the Muslim world. Muslims often pray to Jesus for requests of healing and for prosperity in goods as well as fertility in having many children. Some see Jesus as one who has *baraka,* power.

Thus, the Islam of the Quran views Jesus more formally as a prophet and great human being. The traditions of folk Islam place Jesus in a role of mediator between God and humanity, as a healer, as a protector against evil, and as one who has power to work miracles. The traditions make Jesus more accessible, more personal, and more practical to human desires and needs.

IN SUMMARY OF ISLAMIC AFFIRMATIONS

The most authoritative source for Islam is the Quran. The Quran attributes to Jesus more reverential and honorific titles than to any other prophets including Muhammad. Some are more straightforward like "prophet," "Son of Mary," and "servant." Others are more enigmatic like "word," "spirit," and "messiah."

Jesus is highly praised. He is a miracle worker, a healer, and he raised people from the dead. Basic to the role of Jesus is that he was given the revelation of the Book from heaven called the Gospel (*injil*). It is the same revelation and truth which God gave to Moses in the Torah and which God gave to Muhammad in the Quran.

The death of Jesus is surrounded in somewhat of a mystery as the Quran states that it appeared that he died at the crucifixion. However, God takes him up to Himself. Thus, the Quran is silent on Jesus' resurrection from the tomb but affirms His being taken into heaven.

Christians in the Quran are viewed with some ambivalence. They are affirmed in following a life of prayer. They are warned not to distort the Gospel. They are criticized for their obstinacy in not accepting Muhammad. They are cajoled to follow the true path of God. And they are told that God will ultimately deal with them in the end.

As Islam developed and expanded across cultures, Muslims began to see Jesus in a different light. Folk Islam turned to Jesus not only in his qualities as prophet and teacher but also as mediator, healer, and miracle worker with great power. The name of Jesus assumed personal and supernatural qualities. There were prayers in His name. There were shrines named after Him.

Islam affirms Christianity from its purest expressions in the Quran in the following ways:

- A religion of monotheism, prophets, angels, and sacred book.
- A religion of the practices of prayer, fasting, giving to the poor and needy.
- A religion based on the judgment day and rewards of heaven and hell.
- The great standing of the prophet Jesus and His bringing of the Gospel.

115

WHAT HAS ISLAM GOT AGAINST CHRISTIANITY?

There is no other religion like Islam in its specific and total denial of the major truth claims of Christianity. It disagrees with a vengeance. The Bible is corrupt. The Trinity is abominable. Christians are polytheists believing in three gods. Jesus is only a prophet and a great man but not the Son of God or Savior or Lord.

Jesus did not die on a cross; there was no crucifixion of Jesus. Jesus was not resurrected from the tomb three days after his crucifixion, for he was not crucified. The basic fault of humanity is weakness and lack of correct knowledge to submit to and obey God. There is no original sin.

There is no salvation by grace through faith. God commands and humanity obeys, and God is the final judge. Humanity needs no mediator. The only freedom of religion is the submission under the rulership of Islam and the assumption of a minority status with certain religious rights.

There is no separation of religion and state as long as Islam is the ruling religion. When Islam is not dominant, it lives in a state of jihad, real jihad or in waiting jihad, with the non-Muslim world. Christianity is a religion of colonialism and imperialism and its association with Western secularism makes it corrupt. It is to be regarded with suspicion and distrust.

Thus, the major denials and disagreements which Islam has with Christianity are:

- The present Bible of Christianity is corrupt and is inferior to the Quran.
- Christians are "People of the Book" who follow untruthful doctrines.
- Jesus is not the divine Son of God.
- The teaching of the Trinity is the worst sin.
- Jesus was not crucified and did not die on a cross.
- Jesus was not resurrected from the tomb after the crucifixion.
- Jesus is not the mediator between God and man or the savior of man's sins. Jesus did not atone for the sins of man.

THE BIBLE OF CHRISTIANS IS CORRUPT

The Quran is the sourcebook of Muslims for whatever is true about the Bible, Christianity, Christians, and Jesus. They believe it is the perfect word from God. Whatever is in the Bible of Christians is true only as it does not contradict the data in the Quran.

A firm belief of Islam is that God gave a perfect revelation to the Jews through the Torah and the prophets of the time. Also Christians were given a perfect revelation through the Gospel (*injil*) by the prophet Jesus. That revelation is the same as God gave to the prophet Muhammad in the Quran.

However, both the Torah and the Gospel have been corrupted since their times through distorted interpretations and translations. The present Bible for the most part is untrustworthy and heretical. It must be judged in the light of the Quran.

The Quran has stages of acceptance and rejection of Christians and their scripture. In the beginning Muhammad found more positive things about Christians than Jews. He lumped the Jews with pagans in terms of their enmity but accepted Christians in their qualities of love. (Quran 5:82)

As Muhammad established the Islamic community (umma), he asked both Jews and Christians to accept Islam. If not, they must accept minority status and pay the designated taxes. The Quran indicates that Jews and Christians profess to study the same Book but have nothing solid to stand on. But God will judge them on the Day of Judgment. (Quran 2:113)

Christians are said to have forgotten a good part of the message that was sent them originally from God. And Christians have enmity and hatred among themselves which will be judged also on the Day of Judgment. (Quran 5:14)

In conclusion, Muslims believe that the Gospel (*injil*) spoken of in the Quran is not the New Testament or the four Gospels. It is the Gospel which was revealed to Jesus and which he taught.

Traces of the Gospel are found in the New Testament, and Muslims respect the Bible and the "People of the Book" for these fragments. However, Christianity has perpetuated the corrupt teachings of the Trinity and Jesus as the Son of God and mediator between God and man. It is only in the Quran that the truth about God and Jesus is found.

CHRISTIANS ARE "PEOPLE OF THE BOOK" WHO FOLLOW UNTRUTHFUL DOCTRINES

Numerous references in the Quran refer to both Jews and Christians as "People of the Book." "People of the Book" means that Jews and Christians were recipients of the Torah through Moses and the Gospel (*injil*) through Jesus. They were the perfect revelations to the prophets Moses and Jesus as the Quran was to Muhammad.

However, the scriptures of the Jews and Christians have been corrupted in translations and interpretations. They must be evaluated and accepted in light of the perfect Quran.

"People of the Book" are admonished to associate no partners with God, a direct attack on the Trinity. They are accused of rejecting signs from God and clothing truth with falsehood. They are reprimanded for telling lies against God and misrepresenting the Book with their speaking. (Quran 3:64–80)

In the Quran the word for Christians is *Nasara*. It is found fifteen times, only in the passages of the revelations to Muhammad when he was in Medina. They seem to apply to all kinds of Christians, namely Byzantine, Nestorian, and Monophysite.

The Quran does suggest that all, including Christians, who believe in God and the Last Day and who have lived uprightly will receive their rewards in judgment. (Quran 2:59–62)

Christians are compared to Jews and pagans in their nearness to the true believers who are Muslims. The Quran describes Jews and pagans as people of ill will toward the true believers while Christians are closer in love. Christians are devoted to learning, have renounced the world, and are not arrogant. And when they listen to the revelation from Muhammad, they recognize the truth and desire heaven. The consequences otherwise are hellfire. (Quran 5:82–86)

Various stories in Islamic chronicles have described the prophet Muhammad's contacts with Christians. One tradition reports a Christian cousin of Khadija, the first wife of Muhammad, named Waraqa, spoke of Muhammad as a prophet of the people. Muhammad is said to have talked with Christians from Yemen and Abyssinia.

In the best of views of Muslims toward Christians, the Quran urges Muslims not to dispute with "People of the Book" except in a fair manner. It says that both believe in what has been sent down to each community. "Our God and your God is one." If Muslims and Christians rival each other for good works, God will resolve their differences. That will occur in the Last Judgment. (Quran 29:45–46; 5:48–53)

DENIAL OF THE DIVINITY OF JESUS AND THE TRINITY

Jesus as the son of Mary who is a virgin is affirmed in the Quran. The birth is viewed as a sign from God and as miraculous. Mary is highly regarded. (Quran 3:42–47) The Quran also attributes the title "messiah" to Jesus eleven times. This may be related to Jesus' virgin birth and to his being a prophet of God's word.

The Quran denied Jesus as the Son of God. They commit blasphemy who say that God is Christ the son of Mary. (Quran 5:17) It is not fitting to the majesty of God to beget a Son. A great sin for Islam is to associate the divine nature of God with man. That sin is called shirk.

Islam thus denies any belief in incarnation of God in Christ or the divinity of Jesus as the Son of God. Jesus is a created being. He is compared to Adam in the sense that both were created by God and were without a father. To Muslims belief in a Son of God is an offense against the unity of God. (Quran 112)

The Quran denies the Trinity. It admonishes Christians as "People of the Book" to commit no excesses in their religion by believing that Jesus is more than a prophet from God. Desist from the Trinity. God is far too exalted to have a Son. (Quran 4:171) They commit blasphemy who say that God is one of three in a trinity. (Quran 5:73) Jesus is asked by God if he told men to worship him and his mother as gods in derogation of God. Jesus says that he could never say what he had no right to say. (Quran 5:116)

Muslims erroneously believe that Christians believe in and worship three gods. Popularly, they say the gods are God, Jesus, and Mary. The Trinity is looked upon as polytheism.

JESUS WAS NOT CRUCIFIED ON A CROSS

The major reference in the Quran which refers to Jesus and the crucifixion is: "That they said in boast, We killed Christ Jesus the Son of Mary, the Messenger of Allah but they killed him not, nor crucified him, But so it was made to appear to them, and those who differ, therein are full of doubts with no certain knowledge, but only conjecture to follow, for of a surety, they killed him not. Nay Allah raised him up unto Himself." (Quran 4:156–158)

Muslim scholars themselves have had varying interpretations of this Quranic passage. The reference indicates that Jesus was not crucified and that God planned and made it look like they (the Jews or the Romans) crucified him. Traditional scholarship says that Jesus hid in a niche in the wall, and one of his companions died in his place. Some write that God sent angels to protect Jesus, and Judas Iscariot was made to look like Jesus and took his place.

Some Muslims believe that Simon of Cyrene was substituted while he was carrying Jesus' cross. A traditional view is that the Jews tried to kill Jesus but were unable to do so. They believe that Jesus was taken up into heaven to be with God.

Other Quranic references are to the death of Jesus. One refers to Jesus, speaking that peace is upon him the day of his birth, the day of his death, and the day of his being raised up alive. (Quran 19:33–34) Another has God saying to Jesus that God will bring his life to an end and raise Jesus to himself and purify him from those who have disbelieved. (Quran 3:48–55) These are believed to point to the death of Jesus as being the will of God.

Thus, the Quran states that Jesus was not crucified and that it only appeared that he was. Muslims have some theories about Jesus and the supposed crucifixion but do not suggest or admit that he died on a cross or that his death was connected to the sins of the world or for the atonement of the world.

NO RESURRECTION FROM THE TOMB
AFTER THE CRUCIFIXION

The Quran refers to Jesus, being raised up to God, and one reference states that he was raised up alive. (3:48–55; 4:156–157; 19:33–34) However, nothing in the Quran refers explicitly to the resurrection of Jesus from the tomb. If Jesus never died on the cross, there could be no resurrection of his crucified body from the tomb.

Muslim writers and traditions have reported various stories of the latter days of Jesus. These include that Jesus will return from heaven, battle the Antichrist, and defeat him. Jesus will confess Islam, kill all swine, break all crosses, and establish a millennium of righteousness. There is a tradition that Jesus will marry and have children.

Baidawi, a noted commentator on the Quran and the traditions, has written that Jesus would descend in the Holy Land, would kill the Antichrist, go to Jerusalem, kill the swine and all who would not believe in him, preside over peace for forty years, and then die and be buried in Medina beside the tomb of Muhammad. The Quran says nothing of these traditions although it has indications of Jesus, playing a possible eschatological role. Folk Islam with its various traditions has considered Jesus in a different light than orthodox Quranic Islam.

JESUS: NO MEDIATOR AND BRINGER OF SALVATION

There are numerous references in the Quran indicating that Jesus was prophet, messiah, word and spirit of God, and a sign from God. In fact, Jesus is the only prophet given the titles of messiah, word, and spirit. He was the son of Mary, a virgin. One may say that Jesus is given more honorific titles in the Quran than any other prophet, including Muhammad the final prophet.

However, the Quran condemns any thought that Jesus was the Son of God, the mediator between God and man, the bringer of salvation by his death by crucifixion and his resurrection from the tomb.

The greatest sin in Islam is to associate the nature of God with human nature (*shirk*) as Christianity does in its teachings about the divinity and incarnation of Jesus. Thus, Islam cannot tolerate and it condemns Christian teachings about Jesus as divine and as savior. Man is directly responsible to God without any mediator. Man relies on God for salvation as man keeps the faith and practice of Islam. In the final judgment, God decides destiny between heaven and hell.

RELIGIOUS LIBERTY AND FREEDOM OF RELIGION

On one hand the Quran asserts, "Let there be no compulsion in religion." (2:256) On the other hand it states, "If anyone desires a religion other than Islam (submission to God), never will it be accepted of him, and in the hereafter he will be in the ranks of those who have lost." (3:85)

Islam has a history of ill treatment and at times death to those who leave it. The Quran speaks harshly of apostasy; an apostate will face the wrath of God in the hereafter. (47:25–28) Islamic law (*sharia*) often demanded the punishment of death for apostasy from Islam. Many traditions say of those who change their religion from Islam, "Let them be killed."

Christians have been placed in great danger in missionary efforts toward Muslims. Any convert from Islam to Christianity has also faced even greater risk. Thus, freedom of religion has not been a positive matter within Islam. Some Muslim nations prohibit missionary activity, restrict the religious freedom of minority religions, and place great obstacles in church building and growth.

The overarching worldview of Islam is that of Islam against the world. The world must be converted to Islam or brought under its domination. Islam has favored from time to time Jews and Christians as "People of the Book." If they would not convert, they were given minority status which included prohibition against missionary activity toward Muslims.

The Muslim view has been "once a Muslim always a Muslim," thus the harsh treatment for apostasy. As Islam grows and multiples in non-Muslim populations, it faces the issues of separation of religion and state and religious liberty for all peoples.

CHAPTER 11

CHRISTIAN RESPONSES TO MUSLIM DENIALS

FROM HERE TO ETERNITY

Christians seek their answers to life's problems and to their eternal destiny in the truth of God through biblical revelation. Specifically, they look to the life and teachings of Jesus Christ as presented in the Bible.

The Bible is completely trustworthy on all matters of ethical living, on salvation in the atoning death of Jesus Christ crucified on the cross for the sins of the world, on the resurrection from the tomb, on the ascension of Jesus into heaven, and on all other matters on the reconciliation of the world to God, on judgment of the sins of the world, and on human destiny.

THE BIBLE: THE SOURCEBOOK OF TRUTH AND SALVATION

The Bible is the sourcebook and the authority for Christians on matters of faith and practice. Jesus said, "Heaven and earth will pass away, but My words will by no means pass away" (Matt. 24:35 NKJV).

Muslims have believed that the Torah and the Gospel were perfect as they were originally presented by Moses and Jesus. They castigate the present Bible as corrupt, and they ridicule its many versions as in disagreement with one another. Christians answer that the Bible versions are only different translations which are in harmony with the original

Hebrew Old Testament and the Greek New Testament. There are some two thousand translations in the various languages and dialects of the world.

To Muslims who say that the Bible was corrupted before the time of Muhammad, the Quran asserts, "If thou wert in doubt as to what We have revealed unto thee, then ask those who have been reading The Book from before thee. The Truth hath indeed come to thee from thy Lord. So be in nowise of those who doubt" (Quran 10:95).

In the Quran, God is commanding the Muslims to look back at the scriptures (Book) before the coming of the Quran to ascertain the truth. God certainly would not refer one to a corrupt scripture of the past. The Quran also states, "And dispute ye not with the People of the Book except with means better (than mere disputation), unless it be with those of them who inflict wrong and injury. But say We believe in the Revelation which has come down to you. Our God and your God is One; and it is to Him We bow in Islam" (29:46).

Muslims are also reminded in the Quran that God is the guardian or protector of the holy books. "We have without doubt sent down the Message. And We will assuredly guard it from corruption" (15:9). And the Quran also counsels, "And recite and teach what has been revealed to thee of the Book of thy Lord. None can change His words, and none wilt thou find as a refuge other than Him" (18:28).

Thus, the Muslim is encouraged to believe that God has protected the scriptures which are His truth. If the Muslim considers that the Bible is corrupt, why would he even hold that it prophesies Muhammad? If the Bible is corrupt, then the Muslim may be asked where are the uncorrupt copies of the Bible, that is, the Torah and the *Injil* which God promised to protect?

Christians are told in the Bible, "All Scripture is God-breathed and is useful for teaching, rebuking, correcting and training in righteousness" (2 Tim. 3:16 NIV). And the apostle John writes, "For I testify to everyone who hears the words of the prophecy of this book: If anyone adds to these things, God will add to him the plagues that are written in this book; and if anyone takes away from the words of the book of this prophecy, God shall take away his part from the Book of Life, from the holy city, and from the things which are written in this book" (Rev. 22:18–19 NKJV). Furthermore, the apostle Paul writes, "But even if we, or an angel from heaven, preach any other gospel to you than what we have preached to you, let him be accursed" (Gal. 1:8 NKJV).

Thus, Christians are reminded that Scripture is of God. And Muslims are told, "We believe in Allah, and the revelation given to us, and to Abraham, Ismail, Isaac, Jacob, and the tribes, and that given to

Moses and Jesus, and that given to all Prophets from their Lord. We make no difference between one and another of them. And we bow to Allah" (Quran 2:136).

Jesus said to the Jews who believed him, "If you abide in My word, you are My disciples indeed. And you shall know the truth, and the truth shall make you free" (John 8:31–32 NKJV). The Quran acknowledges the Revelation to Jesus. The Bible states that Jesus not only was the Word but taught the Word. For Christians, the Bible is the guarded and certain revelation of God.

UNITY OF GOD AND SONSHIP OF JESUS IN THE TRINITY

Christianity has stood firmly on its teaching of the Trinity of God the Father, Jesus Christ the Son of God, and the Holy Spirit. It believes in the triune God who reveals Himself as Father, Son, and Spirit. Islam has attacked this belief as polytheism or tritheism.

Muhammad believed the Christian Trinity as follows: "And then God said, O Jesus, son of Mary, did you say to the people, take me and my Mother as two gods apart from God? He said, Glory be to you, I cannot say what is not my right to say" (Quran 5:116). Thus, the Quran says that Jesus himself rejected the Trinity as God, Mary, and Jesus. He did not reject the Christian Trinity of Father, Son, and Holy Spirit.

Both Islam and Christianity believe and teach the unity of God. Both are monotheistic religions. The Bible states, "The LORD our God, the LORD is one!" (Deut. 6:4 NASB). This statement is repeated by Jesus, and the disciples repeat this truth in the New Testament (Mark 12:29; 1 Cor. 8:4, 6). The difference between Christianity and Islam is that Christianity believes there is a plurality of persons or relationships in the unity of the nature of God.

The Bible refers to Jesus as the "only begotten Son" of God (John 1:18; cf. 3:16). Muslims interpret "Son of God" as a physical generation between God and Mary, namely, that God had intercourse with Mary to produce Jesus. Christians interpret "Son of God" as a unique relationship between God and Jesus, in a filial and relational sense rather than a carnal and physical sense.

The Quran reacts to the Sonship of Jesus: "And the truth is that our Lord is exalted, He has not taken a female companion nor a son" (Quran 72:3). "Say God is one, the eternal refuge, He does not give birth, neither is he born, there is no one who can equal him" (112:1–4).

There are two words in Arabic for son, namely, *walad* and *ibn*. The Quran uses *walad* for "son," which means "a physical boy born to parents." Thus, Muslims have believed that Mary gave birth to God or that God had sex with Mary to create the God Jesus.

The Bible describes "Son of God" to Mary: "The Holy Spirit will come upon you, and the power of the Most High will overshadow you; therefore, the child to be born will be called Holy, the Son of God" (Luke 1:35 RSV). Jesus at his birth is called Son of God, and the birth is caused by the coming of the Holy Spirit to Mary. There is no physical intercourse between God and Mary.

The New Testament translation in Arabic uses the word *ibn* for son rather than *walad*. Jesus is called the Son of God, namely, Ibn-Allah, as descriptive of His unique relationship with God the Father. It is a spiritual relationship with God through the Holy Spirit. Jesus later describes this relationship: "I can do nothing on my own authority; as I hear, I judge; and my judgment is just, because I seek not my own will, but the will of him who sent me" (John 5:30 RSV).

Not only does the teaching of the Trinity refer to God the Father and to Jesus Christ the Son, but also it includes the Holy Spirit. The Holy Spirit is revealed in the Bible as follows: as God (Acts 5:3–4); in the act of creation (Gen. 1:2); as omniscient and omnipresent (1 Cor. 2:10–11; Ps. 139:7–12); in the act of salvation (John 3:5–6; Rom. 8:9f; Titus 3:3–5); associated with the names of the Father and Son (Matt. 28:18–20); and in Christian benedictions (2 Cor. 13:14).

There is some mystery to the understanding of the doctrine of the Trinity. It cannot be proven by human reasoning. It is a truth that comes through revelation in the Bible. It speaks to the unity of God and to God's relationships through Jesus and the Holy Spirit to the creation of the world and to the redemption and reconciliation of the world unto Himself.

A wide chasm stands between Christianity and Islam in the teachings of the Trinity and Jesus Christ as the Son of God. Muslims misinterpret and misrepresent Christianity's teachings and understandings. However, Islam holds high Jesus as Son of Mary, as Word of God, as Spirit of God, as Worker of Miracles, and as One honored in this world and the next. "His name is the Messiah Jesus, son of Mary, Honored in this world and the next among those who are close to God" (Quran 3:45).

THE CRUCIFIXION OF JESUS

The crucifixion of Jesus is the great stumbling block between Islam and Christianity. The heart of Christianity resides in the apostle Paul's word:

> Now, brothers, I want to remind you of the gospel I preached to you, which you received and on which you have taken your stand. By this gospel you are saved, if you hold firmly to the word I preached to

you. Otherwise, you have believed in vain. For what I received I passed on to you as of first importance: that Christ died for your sins according to the Scriptures, that he was buried, that he was raised on the third day according to the Scriptures, and that he appeared to Peter, and then to the Twelve. After that, he appeared to more than five hundred of the brothers at the same time (1 Cor. 15:1–6 NIV).

The cross is the crucial belief of Christians. Without the cross there is no resurrection. Without the resurrection, faith is in vain (1 Cor. 15:14). The Quran reports the Muslim denial of the crucifixion:

That they said in boast We killed Christ Jesus the Son of Mary, the Messenger of Allah. But they killed him not, nor crucified him, but so it was made to appear to them. And those who differ therein are full of doubts, with no certain knowledge, but only conjecture to follow, for of a surety they killed him not. Nay, Allah raised him up unto Himself; and Allah is exalted in Power, Wise. (Quran 4:157–158)

Muslims generally interpret the Quranic reference of the appearance of Jesus' crucifixion as God, casting the likeness of Jesus upon Judas Iscariot, Simon of Cyrene, or someone from the gathered crowd who was crucified in his place. Islam has no need of a mediator with God, of a savior who dies for their sins on a cross, and of a resurrected Lord who promises eternal life for the faithful.

But why does Islam take Jesus off the cross? The Messiah Jesus has no role to overcome human sin, for there is no human depravity and no need for salvation. Jesus as the Son of Mary, not the Son of God, has no role in reconciliation and salvation of man to God. Jesus as prophet is not allowed by God to die such a crucifixion, and thus by fate Jesus is freed from the cross. Thus, for Islam there is no need for crucifixion. It denies the crucifixion of Jesus as a fact.

Christianity and history give ample and explicit evidence of the fact of Jesus' crucifixion:

- Old Testament predictions (Isa. 53:5–10; Ps. 22:16; Dan. 9:26)
- Fulfillment of Old Testament prophecies of the coming Messiah in Jesus (Matt. 4:14; 5:17–18; 8:17; John 4:25–26; 5:39)
- Jesus told of His coming death (Matt. 12:40; 17:22–23; 20:18–19; Mark 10:45; John 2:19–21; 10:10–11)

- Predictions of Jesus' resurrection on fact of His death (Ps. 16:10; Isa. 26:19; Dan. 12:2; John 2:19–21; Matt. 12:40)
- Nature of crucifixion leads to death; Mark 15:25, 34 reports loss of blood for more than six hours on the cross; Jesus had to pull himself up to breathe
- Jesus' side was pierced
- John 19:34 reports "blood and water"
- Jesus' act of dying reported (Luke 23:46; John 19:30; Luke 23:47–49)
- Roman soldiers said Jesus died (John 19:33)
- Pilate verified Jesus' death (Mark 15:44–45)
- Report that Jesus was wrapped in cloth and spices (John 19:39–40; Matt. 27:59–60)
- Non-Christian historians of first and second centuries report Jesus' death: Josephus, Tacitus, Thallus, Lucian, Talmud
- Early Christian writers write of death of Jesus: Polycarp, Ignatius, Justin Martyr

BODILY RESURRECTION FROM THE TOMB

The crucifixion of Jesus and His bodily resurrection from the tomb are central beliefs of Christianity. Islam denies both beliefs although it speaks of the death of Jesus and of His being raised up to God.

The Quran states:

"Behold! Allah said, O Jesus, I will take thee and raise thee to Myself and clear thee of the falsehoods of those who blaspheme. I will make those who follow thee superior to those who reject faith to the Day of Resurrection, then shall ye all return unto me" (Quran 3:55). "Allah raised him up unto Himself" (4:158). "So Peace is on me the day I was born, the day that I die, and the Day that I shall be raised up to life again" (19:33).

Muslim writers have given various interpretations to the thought that Jesus was raised up. Traditional Islam has held that Jesus was taken to heaven in a physical body, that he returned to earth after this "ascension" and sent his disciples out, and then returned to heaven to await the judgment.

Tradition has claimed that Jesus would return again and rule as a just king. Some Muslim theories have held that Jesus would return and kill the Antichrist, worship in Jerusalem, kill all swine, rule in peace for forty years, die, and be buried in Medina.

However, the Quran is silent on many of the Muslim traditional ideas about Jesus. It does not affirm that Jesus died on the cross to save men from their sins. And it does not affirm that Jesus was resurrected from the tomb after the crucifixion as victorious over death and ascended into heaven after forty days.

The resurrection of Jesus Christ is at the heart of Christianity. The apostle Paul wrote, "He was raised on the third day according to the Scriptures, and that he appeared to Peter, and then to the Twelve" (1 Cor. 15:4–5 NIV). Paul continues, "If there is no resurrection of the dead, then not even Christ has been raised. And if Christ has not been raised, our preaching is useless and so is your faith" (1 Cor. 15:13–14 NIV).

Christians believe Jesus rose from the dead on the third day after the crucifixion in a transformed physical body. He appeared to more than five hundred of His disciples on twelve separate occasions over a forty-day period. He talked with them and had meals with them.

Before the day of resurrection, many spoke of its coming. Old Testament prophecies were cited with reference to Jesus' resurrection (Ps. 16:8–11 quoted in Acts 2:25–31 in the preaching of Simon Peter).

Jesus also spoke of his coming resurrection. "Destroy this temple [of my body], and in three days I will raise it up" (John 2:19, 21). He said, "As Jonah was three days and nights in the belly of the sea monster, so shall the Son of Man be three days and three nights in the heart of the earth" (Matt. 12:40 NASB). His death and resurrection became a central part of his teaching (Matt. 12:39; 16:4; Mark 8:31; 14:58; Matt. 27:63). Jesus said of His life and the power which He had, "I have the power to lay it down and I have the power to take it up again" (John 10:18 RSV).

Islam says many things about Jesus both in the Quran and in tradition. Jesus Himself is quoted as speaking about the day of his death and the day of his being raised up. However, the Quran is emphatic that Jesus did not die on the cross; it states that it appeared that he did. And the Quran, though it does not deny the resurrection of Jesus, speaks only of His being raised up with little further clarity. Muslims through their traditions have believed many things about Jesus, including His being with God, returning to earth to establish a reign of peace, and His having some role in the last judgment.

The basic beliefs of Christianity reside in the death and resurrection of Jesus, as Jesus, being Emmanuel, God with us, as Jesus dying on the cross for the atonement of the sins of the world, and as Jesus being resurrected from the grave demonstrating victory over sin and the promise of eternal life. Islam denies the Jesus whom Christianity believes.

Salvation in No Other Name

In the preaching of Simon Peter soon after the ascension of Jesus Christ, he tells the people that he stands before them filled with the Holy Spirit and in the name of Jesus Christ of Nazareth who was crucified but whom God raised from the dead. He stated, "Salvation is found in no one else, for there is no other name under heaven given to men by which we must be saved" (Acts 4:12 NIV).

In Christianity, salvation is subsumed under the veracity and integrity of the life, teachings, death, and resurrection of Jesus Christ. Because man was created good by God but fell to temptation by Satan, God sent Jesus Christ to be the mediator, Savior, and reconciler between man and God. The apostle Paul writes, "For it is by grace you have been saved, through faith—and this is not from yourselves, it is the gift of God—not by works, so that no one can boast" (Eph. 2:8–9 NIV). Paul indicates that it is through Jesus Christ that this grace is given.

✳In Islam the view of salvation is one of man, striving (jihad) to please God. The problem of humanity is not rebellion against the will of God but an inherent weakness in human nature to be forgetful or ignorant about the will of God. Muslims must confess the oneness of God, the last prophet Muhammad, and a belief in life after death. "For those who believe and do deeds of righteousness hath God promised forgiveness and a great reward" (Quran 5:9).

At the center of the difference between Christianity and Islam are their teachings on salvation. Islam presents Muslims with no need for a mediator between them and God. There is the straight path of beliefs and practices under the providential will of God. Christianity presents all humanity with a mediator who is the way, the truth, and the life. Jesus said, "I am the way and the truth and the life. No one comes to the Father except through me" (John 14:6 NIV). He also said, "I have come that they may have life, and that they may have it more abundantly" (John 10:10 NKJV).

A Basic Response

Christianity has faced major denials of its central teachings by Islam since Islam's beginning some fourteen hundred years ago. The Quran, itself, has stated the basic denials of Christianity's teachings concerning the Trinity, Jesus as the Son of God, the crucifixion of Jesus, and Jesus' resurrection from the grave. Thus, Islam's view of God, the condition and needs of humanity, the way of salvation, and the role of Jesus have been set against the views of Christianity.

NINE ESSENTIALS OF OUTREACH TO MUSLIMS

1. **KNOW YOURSELF**
   Your Strengths, Your Comfort Levels, The Suitable Contexts

2. **KNOW YOUR FAITH**
   Your Biblical Beliefs, The History and Mission of the Church

3. **KNOW YOUR LORD**
   Jesus Said: "Come unto to me all who labor and are heavy-laden, and I will give you rest."
   "I am the Way, the Truth, and the Life. No one comes to the Father except through Me."

4. **UNDERSTAND THE MUSLIM**
   The Muslim may be a sincere seeker after God who knows Jesus only from the Quran as a Prophet.

5. **UNDERSTAND ISLAM**
   Islam is a monotheistic religion based on a message of prophets and a holy book and required religious practices and a global mission.

6. **UNDERSTAND CHALLENGES**
   There are similarities of words and practices between Christianity and Islam, but there are vast differences of meanings.

7. **SPEAK NATURALLY**
   Meet Muslims and speak with Muslims in words and actions comfortable to you. Friendship and hospitality are treasured by Muslims.

8. **SPEAK EXPERIENTIALLY**
   Your experiences with God and your relationship with Jesus Christ are more powerful in outreach to Muslims than argumentation and debate.

9. **SPEAK BIBLICALLY**
   Pray for yourself and Muslims (2 Chronicles 4:14)
   Love Muslims (1 Corinthians 13; John 13:34)
   Witness to Muslims (2 Timothy 2:24,25; 1 Peter 3:15)
   Give the Scriptures to Muslims

The Word of God's salvation is confession of sin, being repentant, receiving forgiveness, and accepting Jesus Christ as Savior and Lord.

"The Scriptures in the Language of Muslims"
International Bible Society
P.O. Box 62970
Colorado Springs, CO 80962-2970

Since Islam arose some seven hundred years after the birth of Christianity, it responded to Christianity and to the knowledge it had in its own environment. Christianity arose before Islam and therefore did not specifically respond to Islam as such but to the human condition. It did not, for example, mention the prophet Muhammad or Islam. It spoke to the conditions of idols, other religions, false prophets, the figure of Jesus Christ, and the worldview, values, and ways of life which he taught and initiated.

Islam can be appreciated as a global religion of significant influence. Its teachings on monotheism, prophets, angels, scriptures, and judgment can be examined in serious reflection. Its call for daily prayers, a season of fasting, and benevolences to the poor and needy may call one to serious obedience in a religious devotion.

Because Christianity and Islam are missionary religions, they have strong mandates to share their messages and ways with other populations. Muslims have missions to Christians, and Christians have missions to Muslims. There are strong disagreements between the two religions over what each would consider life-and-death matters.

Yet there are many biblical and Quranic sayings which both Christians and Muslims can explore which may bring greater insight into their relationships: for example the God of mercy, justice, and compassion; Jesus as Messiah, Word, and Spirit; Jesus, being raised up to God; patterns of obedience; the ethical and moral life.

Major divisions still exist. Christians do not accept Muhammad as the last prophet. Muslims do not accept Jesus as the Son of God and the crucified and resurrected Christ.

The Quran states, "Those who deny Allah and his Messengers, and those who wish to separate Allah from His Messengers, saying, We believe in some but reject others . . . they are in truth equally unbelievers. And we have prepared for unbelievers a humiliating punishment" (Quran 4:150–151).

The Bible has stated that it is in Jesus Christ that salvation has come to all humanity. Jesus said, "A new commandment I give to you, that you love one another; as I have loved you, that you also love one another. By this all will know that you are My disciples, if you have love for one another" (John 13:34–35 NKJV).

The apostle Paul wrote in the love letter to the Corinthians, "And now these three remain: faith, hope, and love. But the greatest of these is love" (1 Cor. 13:13 NIV). That kind of love was described as patient, kind, unboastful, not self-seeking, not proud, not rude, not easily angered, not keeping a record of wrongs, not delighting in evil. That kind of love always protects, always trusts, always hopes, always perseveres, and rejoices with the truth. A Christian response to Muslim peoples is surrounded by these teachings of Jesus Christ and the apostle Paul because the Christian has been called to follow the Way, the Truth, and the Life.

CHAPTER 12

JESUS AND MUHAMMAD

TWO LEADERS OF WORLD SIGNIFICANCE

Jesus and Muhammad are the founders of two of the world's largest religions whom billions have followed since their beginnings and who now represent nearly half of the global population. The Bible speaks much of Jesus but does not mention Muhammad, who came some seven hundred years later. The Quran speaks much of Muhammad and Jesus as prophets and messengers of the divine revelation of God.

Muslims view the Quran as the divine word becoming a book. It is the perfect revelation from God, and the original book of which the Quran is a recording is with God in heaven. Therefore, what the Quran says about Jesus and Muhammad, as well as about all matters, is authoritative, absolute, and complete.

Christians view Jesus as God's incarnation and the divine word becoming a person. Thus, as Muslims see a book as a perfect revelation, Christians see a person, Jesus, as a perfect revelation. For Muslims, Muhammad is the last prophet, and Jesus is one of the great prophets. For Christians, Muhammad is the founder and leader of a religion called Islam, called a prophet and messenger in the Quran.

There are many similarities between Jesus and Muhammad in their lives, environments, and teachings. They both belong to religious traditions of monotheism, prophets, angels, holy scriptures, and a judgment day with accountability of rewards. Their progenitors are Middle

Easterners, Semitic peoples, and descendants of Abraham. They speak much of prayer and attention to the poor and needy.

There are great dissimilarities between them. They speak differently about God and their relationships to God. They define themselves differently to their followers. They assume quite contrasting roles as religious leaders. Their followers view them in extraordinarily different ways. Literally, their births and their deaths are two opposite stories.

Who do Muslims say that Muhammad is? They say that there is no God but God and Muhammad is the last apostle or messenger of God. He is more to them, of course, but that statement is the confession they make.

Who do Christians say that Jesus is? Jesus posed that question to his disciples: "Who do men say that I am?" Simon Peter answered that some say he is John the Baptist or Elijah or Jeremiah or one of the prophets. Jesus asked once again, "But who do you say that I am?" Simon Peter answered Jesus by saying that he was the Christ, the Son of the living God.

Some one billion and eight hundred million Christians look to Jesus as the founder and inspirer of their religion Christianity. And over one billion Muslims look to Muhammad as the founder of their religion Islam and to Jesus as a noted prophet in their own tradition. Much can be learned from an examination of their lives.[1]

BACKGROUNDS

Jesus was born into an environment of several thousand years of the history of Yahweh God's dealing with the people called Israel. There had been prophets, and priests, and kings in the land of Palestine. At the time of his birth, the Romans ruled the territory, and the Jews with their religion, Judaism, were restless. There were expectations of a messiah and a revolutionary leader.

Muhammad was born in the Arabian peninsula in an environment of tribalism, animism, and polytheism. The tribes revered and worshiped spirits and gods and goddesses. There was a high god called Allah. Surrounding the peninsula there was warfare between the Christian Byzantine Empire in the west and the Zoroastrian Sassanian Empire in the east. The times seemed ripe for change.

BIRTHS

Jesus was born in Bethlehem of Judea about 2 B.C. Prophecies of the Old Testament had pointed to his birth. In the Gospels of Matthew and Luke the story of the birth of Jesus is told. It includes the annunciation by angels to the virgin Mary, the circumstances of the birth in and around Bethlehem, and the visits of the angels and the Magi. An angel appeared to Joseph, Mary's husband, and told him that Mary would conceive a Son through the presence of the Holy Spirit, that his name would be Jesus, and that he would save his people from their sins.

Muhammad was born in Mecca of the Arabian peninsula about A.D. 570. Before his birth, his father, a member of the powerful Quraish tribe, died. His mother, Amina, gave him to Bedouin foster parents to raise near Mecca. After several years he returned to his mother, who died shortly thereafter. His uncle, Abu Talib, cared for him into his adult years.

EARLY LIVES

Jesus grew up in the town of Nazareth in the Galilee region of Palestine. His father was a carpenter. Little is known of Jesus' early life. The Bible reports that he grew strong and was filled with wisdom and that the grace of God was upon him. He did go down to the city of Jerusalem several times in his youthful years. When he was twelve years old, he went with his parents to Jerusalem for the Feast of the Passover. He astonished people with his wisdom as he engaged the teachers in the temple courts.

Muhammad lived as an orphan for much of his youthful life. After his parents' deaths, he lived with his uncle, Abu Talib, who took him on caravan trips to Syria. At age twenty-five, Muhammad married Khadija, a forty-year-old wealthy merchant in Mecca. She provided him the economic security he needed to devote much time to religious concerns. The marriage produced several children who died. They adopted a son, Zaid. Fatima, a daughter, later married Ali, her father's cousin. Ali became one of the first converts to Muhammad's new religion. After Muhammad's death, Ali became the first leader of the splinter Islamic group known as Shiites.

THEIR SUMMONS

Jesus was about thirty years old when he was baptized by John the Baptist in the river Jordan. At the baptism heaven was opened and the Holy Spirit descended on Him like a dove. A voice came from heaven saying, "You are my Son, whom I love; with you I am well pleased" (Mark 1:11 NIV). Thus, Jesus began his ministry. He went into the desert led by the Holy Spirit and for forty days and nights he was tempted by Satan, whom he answered through the Scriptures.

Afterward, at Nazareth he spoke in the synagogue from the scroll of Isaiah: "The Spirit of the Lord is upon me, because he has anointed me to preach good news to the poor. He has sent me to proclaim freedom for the prisoners and recovery of sight for the blind, to release the oppressed, to proclaim the year of the Lord's coming" (Luke 4:18–19 NIV).

Muhammad was forty years old when he began to have certain visions from God. By 610 he had been married fifteen years to Khadija. Her wealth had allowed him to have much leisure. He would go with his wife to the cave outside the city of Mecca known as Mt. Hira for rest. There he began to receive from the angel Gabriel visions which would continue until his death. The visions told him to proclaim the truths which became known as the Quran.

This early vision occurred in the month of Ramadan. Muhammad began to preach against the polytheism and animism associated with tribal life, including his own tribe. He preached that there was only one God (Allah) and that idolatry would lead to hellfire. His summons was to be the last prophet.

THE STORY OF TWO CITIES

Jesus grew up in Nazareth and probably lived there until he was baptized. There he observed Palestinian life lived under the rule of the Roman Empire. Many of his teachings in the parables of the Bible most likely draw from his experiences of home and family and village life. As a young adult he probably observed the details of the crucifixions of prisoners led by carrying their crosses on their backs to a hillside.

Jesus returned to Nazareth after his early desert experience with Satan. After speaking in the synagogue, he said that Scripture was fulfilled by his speaking and presence. He also said that a prophet could not be honored in his own hometown. His hearers drove him out of town.

Jerusalem was the second town of great significance in the life of Jesus. Many times he visited it and preached in its precincts. It was in Jerusalem that he was to face the fury of the Jewish leaders and the power and decision of Pontius Pilate the Roman governor to send Him to be crucified.

His last days were in Jerusalem. He rode in on the back of a donkey with his followers with the crowds singing hosannas. Jesus was arrested, tried, and scourged by the soldiers; he was nailed to the cross and died upon it; he was laid in the tomb of Joseph of Arimathea. He was resurrected on the third day and appeared to the women at the tomb, to his disciples, and to hundreds. After forty days he ascended into heaven.

Before his death Jesus wept over the city, saying how often he would have gathered her unto himself as a mother hen gathers her chicks but they would not. The darkest day and the brightest day in Jesus' life and ministry happened in Jerusalem. It was in Jerusalem that the Holy Spirit came upon his followers, at Pentecost, and sent them on the beginning of a global mission.

Muhammad's fame is associated with two cities, Mecca and Medina, in present-day Saudi Arabia. For the first fifty-two years of his life, he lived in Mecca, the city of his birth. For the last ten years of his life, he lived in Medina, a city some two hundred miles north of Mecca.

It was in Mecca that he grew up in his tribe, married Khadija fifteen years his elder, received the visions from God, preached his newfound message against the idolatry of the tribes of Mecca, and got into deep trouble. He preached monotheism against polytheism and idolatry and an ethic that challenged their traditional ways. In 622 he left Mecca, fleeing from the persecution and death threats upon his life. With his few followers, which included Ali and Fatima, he went to Medina, where he was welcomed by some of the tribes.

In Medina he was given the task of building a community from the factions fighting each other. Muhammad established his religion, Islam, in the community or umma. He assumed the roles of prophet, city ruler, judge, prayer leader of the new mosque he built, and commander in chief of the Muslim armies he organized. When tribes would not submit to his religion and rule, he led his armies against them, killed or subdued them, took booty from them including women as concubines, and attempted to graft them into Islam. Muhammad founded his theocracy at Medina. He also took several wives and concubines.

By 629, he had fought battles against armies from Mecca. By 630 he had returned to Mecca to demand the compliance of the tribes. He cleansed the kaba, known as the house of idolatry, which he had attacked earlier in his preachments in Mecca. He established Mecca as the city of Allah and the city of pilgrimage. In 632 he died from sickness in the lap of his young wife Aisha, whom he had married when she was nine and who had become his favorite wife.

In Islam, Mecca is the most holy city. It is the city that houses the kaba toward which all Muslims face and pray daily. It is the city where all Muslims must come once in their lifetime on pilgrimage to the kaba. Medina is called the city of the prophet. It is where he established the first and true Muslim community. It is the city of Muhammad's tomb and of his great mosque.

For Muslims, Jerusalem is also a holy city. It is the city of the prophet's night journey to heaven to meet Allah. It is also associated with traditions surrounding the prophet Abraham.

POSITIONS ON STRANGERS AND VIOLENCE

Jesus was a Jew. The Jews of the time belittled Gentiles. Jesus related positively to Gentiles and demonstrated love toward them. He healed a psychotic in the Gentile region of the lake of Galilee. He gave

Twenty Topics of Comparison Between Christianity and Islam

Topic	Christianity	Islam
1. Scripture	Bible	Quran
2. God	One God (Monotheism)	One God (Monotheism)
3. Angels	Angels with various functions	Angels with various functions
4. Prophets	Prophets with various functions	Prophets with various functions; Muhammad is final prophet.
5. Jesus	Major titles including Son of God, Savior, Messiah, Lord, Crucified One, Resurrected One	A prophet like other prophets including titles of Messiah, Word of God, Spirit of God
6. Holy Spirit	Part of Trinitarian understanding of God	Spirit of Allah
7. Trinity	Doctrine of God as Father, Son, and Holy Spirit	Vehement denial of Trinity; views Christianity as polytheistic
8. Worship	Private and public; church is community of worship.	Private and public; mosque is community of worship.
9. Leadership	Ordained clergy and laity	formal leaders and laity
10. Sectarianism	Major groups include Roman Catholicism, Eastern Orthodoxy, Protestantism	Major groups include Sunni, Shiite, Sufi
11. Prayer	Individual and community	Required five times daily in regulated ritual; also individual prayer
12. Fasting	Aid in worship	Required yearly during Ramadan

Twenty Topics of Comparison Between Christianity and Islam

Topic	Christianity	Islam
13. Pilgrimage	No requirements	Required once a lifetime
14. Sin	Alienation from God and Resolution in confession, repentance, and forgiveness	Greatest Sin is polytheism (Shirk)
15. Salvation	God gives salvation through grace by faith in relationship to death and resurrection of Jesus Christ	Allah gives salvation with no relationship to the death and resurrection of Jesus
16. Day of Judgment Heaven and Hell	All are realities taught in Bible	All are realities taught in Quran
17. War and Peace	A religion of peace with a history of religious wars	A religion of peace with a history of religious wars
18. Freedom of Religion	Individual freedom with historical examples of intolerance	History and tradition of non-Muslim subjugation and extreme penalties for apostasy
19. Religion and State	History of church and state closeness and separation of church and state	History of Islamic State with minority status of non-Muslims
20. Missions	A missionary religion	A missionary religion

therapy to the daughter of a Greek woman living in Phoenicia, teaching by example that females in a foreign country deserve his concern as well as the males in Palestine. Jesus healed the Roman centurion's son and said he had not observed such faith among his own people. He often said that Gentiles were more acceptable to God in their willingness than the prideful Jews in their narrowness. Jesus loved the stranger and the needy and gravitated toward them, including the hated Samaritans. Jesus commissioned his disciples to go and make disciples of all peoples (*ethna*), excluding none.

Jesus was a peacemaker. He rode into Jerusalem on the back of a lowly donkey, not on a stallion as a warrior carrying a sword. At his arrest in Jerusalem, his disciple Simon Peter impetuously drew his sword to defend Jesus and cut off the ear of a servant of the high priest. Jesus told him to put up his sword, for those who draw the sword will die by it. Jesus did not approve the piety or the plunder of war. He rejected the approach of a "tooth for a tooth." Jesus taught that one should return good for evil by turning the other cheek.

His peacemaking came from his reading of the Isaiah scroll which said that nation should not lift up sword against nation or learn war any more. In his messianic role as the Son of God, Jesus brought a Gospel of peace. He forthrightly and radically demanded that his followers be peacemakers and reconcilers.

He neither formed armies nor led them as commander in chief. Later Christianity used the sword to wage battle against the enemies which it declared. It eclipsed the values which Jesus taught and exemplified and displayed its values of glory, greed, and gore.

Muhammad taught much about meeting the needs of the poor. He also encouraged hospitality toward the stranger. Yet there were admonitions in the Quran to shun those who maintain relationship with Jews and Christians and who take them as friends. Muslims are told they are superior to all other people. Mecca and the kaba became a forbidden territory to non-Muslims.

Slavery was sanctioned by Islam. However, the Quran encouraged the freeing of slaves who showed potential. Muhammad did not condemn slavery nor was he an abolitionist. He himself was a slaveholder.

With regard to violence and war, Muhammad began in Mecca with his preaching of a policy of nonviolence. It was appropriate, for his group was small and his adversaries were large tribes. He might have faced annihilation if he had been militant. He encouraged his followers to return evil with good and to show patience. The basic meaning of jihad, sometimes called the greater jihad, is to strive inwardly to please God in faithfulness and obedience.

About the time of the flight from Mecca to Medina and during the early days in Medina, Muhammad received newer revelations. Muhammad counseled his fledgling followers and forces to fight and kill for God's sake but not to attack first. Yet he declared that oppression is worse than killing.

Muhammad said through the Quran, "The punishment of those who wage war against Allah and His Messenger, and strive with might and main for mischief through the land is: execution, or crucifixion, or the cutting off of hands and feet from opposite sides, or exile from the land. That is their disgrace in this world, and a heavy punishment is theirs in the hereafter" (Quran 5:33).

After Muhammad established his religion and developed a strong community in Medina, he expanded the meaning of jihad. He told his armies through the Quran that it was not they who killed the Meccans in the Battle of Badr but it was God who killed the enemy (8:17). He advocated to strike the necks of the unbelievers until they were defeated. He counseled that those followers who lost their lives in battle for God would be admitted to paradise (47:4, 6; 8:65).

Whereas Muhammad started out in Mecca preaching tolerance and returning good for evil, in Medina he counseled to fight in defense of first attacks upon Muslims. With the buildup of his community and his armies and his sights on capturing Mecca, he moved to a more aggressive holy war.

Muhammad told his followers that the greater jihad was individually to please God. He also told them that the lesser jihad was necessary when the Muslim community went to warfare on behalf of Allah. Muhammad himself was both commander in chief of his forces as well as a warrior.

LOVE GOD AS FATHER, OBEY ALLAH AS OMNISCIENT

Jesus was asked which was the greatest of the commandments. He answered that one should love God with all the heart and soul and mind. And he said that the second commandment was to love one's neighbor as oneself. Jesus taught that God was omniscient and omnipotent. God was Spirit. God was merciful and forgiving. God was Judge. God was described by many other high and noble characteristics.

In both his teaching and in his devotional and prayer life, Jesus often referred to God as love and as Father. He taught his disciples to pray, "Our Father in heaven . . ." (Matt. 6:9 NIV). He said that he and the Father were one. He told the disciples that he who had seen him had seen the Father. He also stated that no one comes to the Father except through himself. And from the cross, Jesus said, "Father, forgive them for they do not know what they are doing." Jesus had a filial relationship to God as His loving Father.

Jesus was the embodiment of God's love. He and His Father were one. His love was God's love. He told his followers to love. Next to the priority of loving God was loving one another and one's neighbor as oneself.

Muhammad concentrated on the unity of God in the midst of the polytheism of his day. The ninety-nine beautiful names of God developed in Muslim piety. At the beginning of the chapters in the Quran the words occur, "In the name of Allah, Most Gracious, Most Merciful."

The titles for God used in the Quran are many, and the most frequently used are The Omniscient (158 times); The Forgiving (96); The Wise (95); The Unique (89); The Mighty (44); and The One (21). There is little reference in the Quran on God being the God of love.

Muhammad, in speaking the revelations of the Quran, describes God more in terms of his law and will and less in his personal nature and essence. Directions are given more to know the laws and will of God and not God Himself; to follow and obey his commandments more than to be involved in any personal relationship to God. There is no language of God being a Father who loves his Son and his children. Much emphasis is placed upon the unity of God, the oneness of God, and not a relationship to God. *Islam* means "submission," and *Muslim* means "one who submits."

A DAY OF JUDGMENT IS COMING

Jesus spoke of both the present and the future. There was an urgency to heal the sick, to restore the sight of the blind, to teach the beatitudes, to condemn greed, and to seek justice and mercy. He spoke harshly of legalism and praised the love ethic.

His teaching the parable of the Good Samaritan indicated the importance of being a good and concerned neighbor. The parable of the Prodigal Son demonstrated God as a father who goes to any limit to love and be reconciled to his children.

Jesus often spoke not only of the coming of the kingdom of God and its nearness but also of the coming end of the world and a great judgment that would result in one's eternal presence in heaven or hell. Heaven is the place where one who followed Jesus would spend an eternity. There would be fellowship with God. There would be no need for marriages. All would be with God. On the other hand, hell was a place of separation from God for eternity.

Jesus said the kingdom of God was at hand. He asked his followers to pray that the kingdom might come. He warned of the coming end of the world and all its consequences. Jesus taught that he was going to prepare a place for eternity and would return to receive those unto Himself. However, he said that no one knows the time of the end, and he emphasized the foolishness of attempting to set exact times and dates. One should work while there is day, for the night is coming. Jesus said to be ready at any time.

Muhammad also spoke of present conditions. The Quran calls people to follow the straight path. The straight path consists of correct beliefs and correct practices. Jews and Christians were often criticized for their waywardness. Especially Christians were condemned for their misplaced beliefs in Jesus as a god and as the Son of God.

Muhammad also presented the coming day of judgment and the day of resurrection. It would be a time of the weighing of one's deeds. Rewards resulted in a paradise, and penalties sent one to hellfire. Paradise in particular was described as a place of great luxury. Spouses will be together with their children. A special pleasure for men is the availability of virgins. Hell is a despicable place of scorching winds and intense heat. Some torture is indicated with precious metals of those who horde them heated and their bodies branded with them.

Muhammad was a warner of things to come. The threat of hell is given more attention in the Quran with 367 verses than heaven which is mentioned in 312 verses. Muslim tradition has stories of the return of Muhammad and Jesus to assist in ending the world and to be present at the great judgment day.

Thus, the present was presented as a time to be warned to follow God's instructions. Muhammad himself served as the excellent example for following the straight path. One should strive for paradise and trust God that one's deeds in the present would be sufficiently good to weight the scales toward paradise.

THEIR ROLES IN CHRISTIANITY AND ISLAM

Jesus assumed many roles in his life of ministry and teaching. He was given many titles by his disciples and early followers in the Bible. Those titles include:

Alpha and Omega	Amen
Ancient of Days	Bread of Life
Counselor	Eternal Life
Friend of Sinners	God our Savior
Good Shepherd	I Am
Image of the Invisible God	Judge of Living and Dead
King Eternal	Life
Light	Living Bread

Lord	Mediator
Messiah	Mighty God
Only Begotten of the Father	Our Passover
Our Peace	Prince of Peace
Prophet	Priest
Redeemer	Righteous Judge
Savior	Son of God
Truth and Grace	Way
Word of God	Word Made Flesh

Jesus in Christianity is believed to be the suffering servant forecast in the Book of Isaiah. He is the promised Messiah, the Son of God, Emmanuel—God With Us, the Savior and Lord. Later Christianity named churches after him, and families named their sons after him.

Muhammad is spoken of in the Quran as follows:

Holy Prophet	A Mercy from Allah
Warner	Seal of the Prophets
Messenger of Allah	Witness
Son of Abd Allah	A Preacher

The Quran states that Muhammad was no more than a messenger. Yet in the Quran, Muslims are encouraged by Muhammad to follow him if they love God, and then God will forgive their sins. Also it is said that he who obeys Muhammad obeys God. In this way devotion to God was closely associated with allegiance to Muhammad.

After Muhammad's death, Muslim tradition continued to elevate him to be the example of human perfection and possibly more. Many of his relics, including hairs, teeth, sandals, his prayer rug, and a sword hilt, are cherished in shrines and are given veneration. His name is the most common one given to male Muslims. Often, Muslims offer intercessory prayers to Muhammad, mosques and shrines are named after him, and miracles are ascribed to him.

CHAPTER 13

THE CHRISTIANS ARE COMING!

A MANDATE AND A MISSION

Christianity is a religion with a mandate and a mission. In some two thousand years Christianity has become a part of the lives of over 1.8 billion people upon every continent. The mandate has been to take the Gospel to all peoples: some atheists, some agnostics, and many members of the great world religions. The mission has been to take the good news of Jesus Christ for salvation, healing, and reconciliation.

Until the latter half of the twentieth century, the religion Islam and the Muslim peoples had been basically neglected by the mission of Christianity. Islam is the second most populous religion with over one billion followers.

Recently, church mission agencies have renewed interest in Muslim peoples. Strategies have been developed for outreach to Muslim people groups, and workers have been sent out especially to Africa, Southeast Asia, South Asia, Central Asia, Europe, and the Middle East. Muslim people groups may be in the geographical area of a nation or may be present across various territories. Examples of such groups are the Kurds in the Middle East and the Fulani across Africa.

THINGS OF THE PAST

Relationships between Christianity and Islam and between Christians and Muslims have had a checkered history. Both have viewed each other often with suspicion, distrust, and sometimes hostility.

Christians have felt that Muslims have misunderstood and misinterpreted Jesus and have labeled Christians as polytheists and the greatest of sinners. Muslims have felt that Christians have never been accepting of Muhammad as prophet and the Quran as revelation from God and have accused Muslims of paganism and savagery.

The past has seen wars and rumors of wars between Christians and Muslims. The era of the Crusades in the Middle Ages stands out as a bitter and bloody warfare between Christian armies and Muslim armies over rights and privileges of the land of Palestine and the city of Jerusalem.

In recent times both have fought each other with their armies in Lebanon and eastern Europe. Christian Armenia has fought Muslim Azarbaijan in central Asia. Aftermaths of the Iranian revolution saw the founding of the Islamic Republic of Iran and the persecution and death of several prominent Iranian Christian pastors as well as much of the Baha'i leadership. Christians and Muslim groups have been fighting in Indonesia—fighting which has resulted in deaths.

The foundations of the life and teachings of Jesus Christ rest in the concepts of agape love (unselfish love) and peace. Although Christianity has not always demonstrated those concepts, it is called upon to do so. Thus, its mandate and mission to Muslims are to be messengers of the agape love and peace of Jesus Christ. The battles which Christians are urged to wage are those of truth, righteousness, patience, and love.

WHAT CHRISTIANS NEED TO KNOW ABOUT ISLAM

Islam is a religion of 1,400 years of history, civilization, and growth. Muslims are proud of their heritage. Serious Muslims desire not only that their religion be understood and appreciated by outsiders but also that non-Muslims consider its merits sufficient enough to accept and practice it.

In meeting and conversing with Muslims, Christians may be helped in knowing the following:

- Muslims are either born into Islam or convert to Islam. They identify their religion with culture.
- The most important words a Muslim may say are, "There is no God but Allah, and Muhammad is the Messenger of God."
- Muslims believe in angels, prophets, scriptures, and a day of judgment. They practice prayers, almsgiving, fasting, pilgrimage, and missions.
- Although Muslims have a uniformity in beliefs and practices, they also have theological differences and practices which separate

them often into competing groups. Examples are Sunni, Shiite, Ahmadiya, Nation of Islam.

🕮 Four issues have great influence upon the attitudes of Muslims toward Christians:

1. Muslims assume that Christians believe in three gods (the Quran teaches the Trinity to be composed of God, Mary, and Jesus; it rejects Jesus as the Son of God.)
2. Muslims believe that Jews and Christians have changed the Old and New Testaments to conceal the predictions of the coming of Muhammad.
3. Muslims believe that Jesus did not die on the cross but that someone took his place.
4. The Crusades have indelibly branded in Muslim memory a continuing attitude that Christianity is a warring religion and Christians are a colonialistic people.

🕮 Muslims believe they have a high concept of Jesus from the Quran when they call him prophet, messenger, messiah, word, and spirit.

🕮 Muslims often view Western nations and peoples as both Christian and colonialist. Consequently they see Christian missionaries as agents of Western Christian governments.

🕮 Muslims may accept popular ideas about Jesus that go beyond the teachings of the Quran. They may view Him as saint and mediator and offer prayers to Him.

🕮 Muslims worldwide identify with the plight of the Palestinians for a homeland and for the return to them of the rights and privileges over the Muslim holy places in Jerusalem.

🕮 Muslims believe they have the best institution for the family with women and children protected. They do not like criticism leveled against the place of women in Islam or their wearing of the veil.

🕮 Muslims do not like films, cinema, or writings they view as caricatures or blasphemy of their prophet Muhammad.

🕮 Muslims criticize the "Christian West," especially the United States, for its corrupt values portrayed in movies and mass media in violence, nudity, and sexual immorality.

🕮 Muslims love to give and receive hospitality with family and friends, especially hospitality centered around food, meals, and festivities.

🕮 Serious Muslims do not drink alcoholic beverages or eat pork products or engage in gambling activities.

🕮 Orthodox Muslims who take seriously their Quran believe their religion is superior to all others in beliefs and practices.

🕮 Muslims believe they have an obligation and a mission to extend their religion until it becomes dominant. There is the world of Islam, and there is the world of ignorance and disobedience. Jihad is their mandate and mission.

Muslims are a proud religious people. Christians are well served in their relationships with Muslims to know their basic beliefs and practices as well as their views about life in general. Christians need to be realistic about the feelings which Muslims may have toward Christianity in particular and toward Christians in general.

It is important to remember that Muslims are like Christians who face life-and-death matters, who laugh and cry, and who desire a better world for themselves and their families. To know a Muslim is to know a fellow traveler through life. If there is basic distrust and suspicion, a Christian can be both understanding and truthful.

EVANGELISM AND ISLAM

A Christian unapologetically is a witness for one's faith. One speaks the truth in love. One shares the Gospel which is the life and message of Jesus Christ. That message includes His crucifixion upon the cross and His resurrection from the tomb. The meaning of the message is that He died for the sins of the world; that He forgives sinners who confess their sins and accept His grace; and that His resurrection is positive proof of the overcoming of sin and the gift of eternal life.

Islam offers many beliefs and practices which are similar to those in Christianity. It also affirms crucial ideas and practices which are antithetical to those in Christianity. An appropriate and decisive evangelism to Muslims is based on the following:

🕮 The message and life of Jesus Christ

🕮 A clear knowledge of Islam

🕮 An appreciation of the challenges and struggles of Muslim peoples

🕮 A love for individual Muslims and their families

🕮 A presentation of biblical truths

🕮 And a sharing of one's own Christian faith

Methods and styles of evangelism to Muslims may differ according to needs, circumstances, and personalities. Especially with much history of uncongenial relations between Christianity and Islam, it is wise to tread carefully but deliberately and intentionally. If one speaks with the tongues of men and angels and has not love, it not only sounds awful but is a disgrace. There are do's and do not's or positive and negative ways of communicating and being present with Muslims.

Don'ts

- Do not accentuate the negative at the beginning of a conversation at the expense of the positive. It may be much better to discuss the meaning of Messiah and Word of God and Spirit of God, as Jesus is given those titles in the Quran, than to start with Jesus as the Son of God and as part of the doctrine of the Trinity, which the Quran condemns. Deeper conversations about these truths may follow.
- Do not demean Islam, the Quran, and Muhammad in a disparaging spirit, for time will provide these topics to be addressed.
- Avoid argumentation and hostile disputes.
- Do not relate one-on-one and alone with the opposite gender unless the cultural norms would permit it and others would completely understand it.

Do's

- Honor and respect Muslims as people with religious beliefs and feelings and culture.
- Cultivate relationships with Muslims by discussing common and similar areas of interest such as belief in one God, the virgin birth, and the names and titles given to Jesus in the Quran.
- Learn Muslim social customs, especially the roles of men and women, greetings and diet, so that embarrassments may be minimal in interactions.
- Include Muslims in activities where they may feel comfortable and may interact with Christians in social and some religious occasions.
- Speak the truth in love. Use parables of Jesus and stories of the healing of the sick and miracles. Include one's own personal witness of what it means to be a follower of Jesus.
- Be prepared to have much patience and perseverance in discussing the truths of the Bible with Muslims and sharing with them the meanings of Jesus as the crucified Messiah and as the resurrected Lord. Prayer and the presence of the Holy Spirit are to be sought as close companions.

Presence and Place

Islam is a religion of worship and prayer. Muslims may pray any-where at the stated daily times. They are encouraged to pray with others in the mosque and to hear the weekly sermon on Fridays.

Although Christians may go to mosques and meet Muslims, more often Christians see Muslims in the workplace or on social occasions in homes or around recreational activities. Muslims, like any other peoples, enjoy hospitalities in the exchange of visits.

Passages of life are critical and important times in the life of Muslims. Birth, marriage, and death are events when one may show concern and support. In expressions of genuine happiness at a Muslim wedding or in sympathy and condolences at the time of a Muslim death, a Christian may become more deeply involved in friendship and may in time be sought for counsel and for the sharing of one's faith.

Presence, or being there with people, may demonstrate a kind of nonverbal behavior which entrusts one to a Muslim and which deepens the way for respect and trust. Words which may not be expressed initially may be spoken in time and in other places.

Proclamation

Evangelism is telling the Gospel. There are many ways and methods. It may be to large crowds, to small gatherings, to a family, or to an individual. In the history of relations between Christians and Muslims, Christians have spoken to Muslims for the most part in smaller groups or as individuals. There have been few large crusade meetings where an evangelist preached to a host of Muslims. In predominant Muslim communities it would not be permitted or appropriate.

A general guideline for evangelism among Muslims is to say and do what is most appropriate for understanding and acceptance of the Gospel, given the conditions and relationships involved. To speak the truth in love is the basis for proclamation. One does not want to compromise the Gospel, nor does one want to forfeit the opportunity to speak the Gospel to Muslims based upon a careless way or method.

Knowing that Muslims are adamant in their denials of certain central beliefs of Christianity and may become argumentative and cut off further discussions and relationships, one can choose to speak about the Gospel in other areas. One may return to these topics of Muslim denial in time.

Proclamation may revolve around the following themes:

🕮 Muslims know the names of many Old Testament prophets and patriarchs from their readings in the Quran. Abraham is a favorite. One may speak of Abraham and figures like him with stories from the Bible, realizing Muslims trace their descent from Ishmael, not Isaac.

- Muslims read of Jesus (Isa) in the Quran and know the highly honorable titles He is given. These titles include Son of Mary, Messiah, Word of God, Spirit of God, Servant of God, Prophet of God, Messenger of God, and others. Many of these most respectful titles are not ascribed to other prophets, including Muhammad. One may inquire of the Muslim why and how Jesus is called Messiah and Word of God and Spirit of God. One may tell of the meaning of Jesus with these terms in the Bible. One may then tell of what these terms mean to one's faith.

- Muslims know that in their Quran Jesus is described as performing miracles, healing the sick, and raising the dead. Their prophet Muhammad is not given to miracles. One may tell the biblical stories of the miracles of Jesus including sight to the blind, the lame walking, and raising of the dead. God is glorified. Often they are told to go and sin no more.

- Narratives and stories which Jesus told, such as the parables, often strike the interest of Muslims, as well as His teachings of the Beatitudes.

- Some Muslims have been exposed to various layers of cultural traditions upon their Islam. Some have been taught or heard stories about Jesus that are not in the Quran. They are interested in the light which Jesus brings or His love from God, like the Muslim Sufis. Some have heard of the power of Jesus and seek His aid in crises and distress, like folk Islam. Some, like the Shiites, see their Imams Ali and Husain as more than saints to whom they voice their prayers and who they say have suffered vicariously for them. Using terms they may more readily understand, one may speak of Jesus as the messiah who came as the Suffering Servant who takes away the sins of the world

- At some point in evangelism one approaches the Muslim with the very personal question, "What do you think of Christ?" Discussions about what the Muslim knew about Jesus in the Quran may have been helpful. But the groundwork for this question may very well have been laid in building trustful relationships, and in talking about suffering and healing, about sinning and guilt and forgiveness, about the power of Jesus not only to heal the body but to forgive sin, about His very visible and physical and historical crucifixion with its meaning of atonement, and about his physical resurrection from the grave with its meaning of the defeat of sin and death and the promise of eternal life.

A Witness Is Not a Warfare

The era of the medieval Crusades is a stigma upon the history of Christianity. It was a time of the clash of Christianity and Islam. The present times call for a witness of Christians who beat their swords into plowshares and who take the helmet of salvation and the sword of the Spirit, which is the Word of God.

Christians know that there is warfare with the evil one of the principalities and powers of the world. They also know that Jesus the Prince of Peace came in selfless love. In relationships with Muslims and in the proclamation of the Gospel, Christians are to speak the truth in love.

MUSLIMS AND THE CHURCH

Traditionally, in Muslim societies a Muslim is born a Muslim. Islam pervades all of life: individual, family, community, and often nation. If one chooses to leave Islam for another religion, it is looked upon as apostasy with serious consequences. There may be excommunication and dismissal from one's family and community. Sometimes there is a penalty of death. A family and a community lose face when one of their own converts to another religion. They consider it a decision made against their God and the family and the community.

Thus, when a Muslim chooses to become a Christian and to be identified with a church, it is a crucial decision with wide ramifications. The decision affects the individual, the family, the Muslim community, the Christian enablers or witnesses, and the church that receives the convert.

The areas of concern include:

- The Muslim convert and challenges of transition
- Safety and protection for all involved
- The time and place of baptism
- Discipling into the church
- Contextualization

The Muslim Convert and Challenges of Transition

The challenges a Muslim faces in choosing to become a Christian are many. One's understanding of Jesus Christ and the conversion experience is a very personal matter as well as one of education and nurturing in the church. There are major transitions from Islamic beliefs and culture to Christian beliefs and church. Time is necessary for education and training in the church.

There is a major change from one's Muslim family and community life. In traditional settings, a Muslim convert must deliberate over when, how, and what will be told family and friends about his decision. Often a considered judgment must be made by the convert of the consequences which may come upon revealing one's decision. One must be ready to leave home and community and to face ridicule and possible persecution.

The church or Christian community into which the convert enters must be prepared. Often the motives of both the convert and the Christians are under examination. The convert may feel that one is a trophy or specimen of an unusual happening. One may also feel in some settings that because a job or some security is offered that one is being bribed to make a decision. On the other hand, Christians may question the motive of the convert in terms of becoming a Christian in order to flee a situation or to find gold at the end of the rainbow in some Christian community or land.

The circumstances for the Muslim convert are usually quite difficult and often dangerous. All concerned must work together in trustful and prayerful relationships.

Safety and Protection for All

In traditional Muslim families and societies, a decision to leave Islam for Christianity is often considered apostasy. One's family ties are severed, and one is asked to leave. The family is scandalized and loses face in the community. Some converts are killed or are under penalty of death. Christians who have facilitated the convert's decision also may be in danger of hostilities since they are seen as outsiders and intruders.

Questions arise concerning safety and protection for all. Christianity has a history of martyrs who have faced hostilities and death in evangelizing and witnessing. It is a possible fact of Christian life, and one does not court protection and security at the expense of the denial of faith. However, one is wise to anticipate possible threats to the life of the convert and Christians and to consider ways to lessen them.

Who is accountable and responsible in the decision-making of the convert? The convert needs to be sensitive in the timing and the ways one communicates the decision to family and friends. It may be gradually as one continues to learn and grow in the new faith. The church or Christian community needs to be patient and understanding of the transition and not to make demands which may unnecessarily imperil the convert's life.

For example, the convert might talk more with his family at the beginning of his conversion about Jesus (Isa) the Messiah and Word of God, and the Christians may leave the time and place of baptism of the convert open. There is a season for everything. Thus, issues of safety and protection are important and may be considered with prayer and common sense by both the convert and the Christians.

Time and Place of Baptism

Baptism is the event for a Muslim convert that normally signifies the official break from Islam. In some Muslim settings if it is done publicly, it may elicit the persecution of the convert and hostility toward the Christians. Baptism usually happens after one's experience and knowledge as a Christian have grown and matured and have been evaluated by other Christians.

Thus, the time of baptism may vary according to the individual and the church. Some Muslim converts desire to have baptism quickly. Others request it to be delayed until family members are given an opportunity to understand the changes in the convert's life. Churches often have a study program over a period of time for the convert to confirm one's life experiences in the new faith.

The place of baptism may be quite public in the church or a river setting, depending on the circumstances surrounding the convert's life. Some request a private baptism with Christians and a few close friends. This baptism has been called a "secret baptism" so as not to alarm the Muslim community.

The ceremony of baptism is highly symbolic of the change from death to the old life to newness of life. It is following the example of Jesus Christ and His teaching to be baptized. It is an act of obedience. Thus, when the Muslim convert is baptized, it is seen not only as leaving his old religion, but it is also seen as assuming a new life in Jesus Christ.

A delay in baptism may be entirely appropriate on both the convert's and church's behalf. It may be feasible to have a baptism which includes several Muslim converts, thus reinforcing their experiences together. Baptism may be a sensitive matter in the life of a former Muslim and the church. It should be approached carefully in prayer and with the well-being of all concerned.

Discipling into the Church

The Muslim convert comes out of a background of very formal worship and prayer in the mosque, of recitations from one's sacred Quran, usually in Arabic which may not be one's native language, and of a highly exacting daily and monthly calendar of rituals and observances. One will be introduced to the singing of hymns and to a variety of patterns of worship quite different from the uniform ritual of the mosque.

The convert will learn about the informality and spontaneity of prayer in the Christian manner from the highly formalized and uniform prayers said five times daily in Islam. One will be taught the model prayer which Jesus offered addressing God as Father. And one will focus more on the weekly activities in the church and on the birth of Jesus at Christmas and His death and resurrection at Easter than on the fasting month of Ramadan and the pilgrimage to Mecca as observed in Islam.

The church will teach the convert its major doctrines. The Book of Psalms will assist in support during times of persecution and hostility. The parables which Jesus taught in the Gospels will be inspirational. The Gospel of John, Hebrews, and James will give one insights. The Acts of the Apostles will give one the history and experiences of the early disciples in launching out in new experiences led by the Holy Spirit. The convert can easily identify his or her own experiences with the emerging church.

One will be discipled from believing Jesus as only a messenger in the Quran to the promised Messiah who is Savior and Lord of Christians; from a life based upon much ritual and ceremony and laws to be fulfilled as commanded in the Quran to a life based on faith and grace and love which becomes the new commandment by Jesus; and from a confession that Muhammad is the last prophet to a confession acknowledging sin and seeking forgiveness.

Contextualization

Contextualization is applying the Gospel appropriately to the culture of the recipients and its reception without violating biblical norms. God sent His Son into the world, the Word becoming flesh and dwelling among the people full of grace and truth.

There is much to think about Christ and His relationship to culture. He judged parts of it. He affirmed some of it. And He came as the transformer of culture, saying that the kingdom of God was present and that it was to come.

The apostle Paul said that he had become all things to all men that he might win some. He went into the marketplace in Athens, mixed with the merchants and philosophers on their home turf, affirmed that they were very religious, and then told them of Jesus and the resurrection.

In the Muslim context, issues for evangelism and church planting have arisen concerning contextualization. What, if any, Muslim beliefs and practices may be brought over into the Muslim convert's new life as a Christian?

Since Islam is based on monotheism, prophets, sacred scriptures, angels, and a judgment day, what, if any, of these beliefs may inform the convert's Christian experience? And since Islam requires the practices of confession, prayer, fasting, almsgiving, and pilgrimage, what, if any, of these meanings or forms may be included in the convert's Christian practices?

The church, its missionaries, and its mission strategies are at variance on these matters. Converts, themselves, differ too. Some say that certain forms of worship which are culturally Islamic may be used by Muslim converts filled in with Christian values and meanings. Others say that any use of Islamic forms would be syncretism.

Contextualization in the Muslim environment has included the building and architecture of the mosque as a worship center, using the Quranic name of Jesus (Isa), employing the Muslim forms of prayer, and observing the fasting season.

Muslim converts have referred to the church as Isa (Jesus) mosques. The architecture is similar to the regular Islamic mosque. There is a *mimbar* (pulpit), small stands for the holding of the open Bible, and rugs on the floor for seating.

There are no pews or chairs. Worship is to God through his Son Jesus with the Bible as the authoritative Word and with the worshipers seated in rows facing the pulpit. The sermon may be given by the preacher from the pulpit.

The name of Jesus in Quranic Arabic is Isa. Isa is the name used for the mosque. It is Isa who is referred to in the Bible. Isa is addressed in prayers. The converts are the followers of Isa.

The Islamic forms of prayer are utilized. During group or individual prayers in the mosque, one sits on the floor by oneself or in a row with others. One stands and kneels while repeating prayers to Isa with expressive hands in front of one and to one's ears following the Islamic tradition. One may face Jerusalem in prayers in place of the Islamic tradition of facing Mecca.

During the Ramadan month of fasting, from sunrise to sunset in the Islamic tradition, the convert may continue the observance, remembering Jesus' teaching and experience in fasting. It is observed to glorify God and to follow the example of Jesus.

Both recent Muslim converts and their Christian compatriots have followed certain of these examples of contextualization. Some have found great meaning in them and have stated that they serve as means of aiding Muslims in their transition to becoming Christian. Other have said that they borrow too much of the Islamic heritage and contaminate the true meanings of what is Christian. The discussions continue of the appropriateness of any cultural transfer of one form or institution to another.

ENCOUNTERS OF THE TWENTY-FIRST CENTURY

Christianity has become a religion of prominence and numbers outside its traditional power-base of Europe and the United States. Western Christianity is becoming subsumed under the growing Christian numbers in Latin America and Africa and Asia. The future portends that the churches in these areas will face the challenge of Islam as both Christianity and Islam grow.

Christianity in the Western nations also faces a surge of Islamic growth. Particularly in western Europe and the United States, Muslims have migrated especially from North Africa, the Middle East, and South Asia. Islam has become a religion second only to Christianity in numbers and influence in many of these countries.

Some challenges that face Christians and the church include the following:

Wars and Rumors of Wars

Jihad has continued to be an arm of Islam. Leaders of nations, namely the late Ayatollah Khomeini of the Islamic Republic of Iran, and dissident factions within Islam have called for jihad against nations and individuals. In the Islamic Republic of Sudan, some 1.9 million people have been killed in the last twenty years in civil war between the Islamic government in the north and the largely Christian rebels in the south. The threat of jihad has continued to be a weapon of certain Muslims against non-Muslims as well as among Muslims who think each other are religiously and politically incorrect.

Permission Denied

Christianity often is persecuted and/or denied freedoms of worship and religious community when it is a minority within a predominantly Islamic environment. Churches are not allowed nor are expatriate missionaries permitted visas for entrance. The Kingdom of Saudi Arabia allows no churches on their soil nor any Christian missionaries permission to enter the country.

The Medina Model of Muhammad and Politics

The form of governance and politics exemplified under the prophet Muhammad in Medina from 622 to 632 is an ideal state model for many

Muslims. It integrated the political, cultural, religious, and military functions of a society under Muhammad, who was a theocrat. He spoke and acted in the name of God following the perfect expression of the commands of God in the Quran.

In that time Jewish tribes were killed off, Christians became sub-servient under the rule of Islam, and Islam acted upon the basis of its superiority and non-Muslim inferiority. Throughout Islamic history, the Medina model has served as an ideal for governance. It has seldom found expression in a total political reality.

However, where Islam has been the great majority of the popula-tion, and where orthodox Islam has had authority and the power of influence to effect its programs, the Medina model has been attempted in its various parts. The Kingdom of Saudi Arabia, the Islamic Republic of Iran, and the Islamic Republic of Sudan are examples which have reflected parts of the Medina model.

The challenges for Christianity from the implementation of this Medina model include:

- Possible hostilities and warfare between Christians and Muslims
- Denial of freedom of religion among Christians in worship, edu-cation, and the building and expanding of churches
- Denial of entry of expatriate Christians in missionary standing with their churches
- Possible introduction of laws which discriminate against minority groups and human rights
- The reinforcement of laws and penalties of the changing of one's religion and apostasy

Responses of Christianity to Muslim Inquiry

Muslims may be prepared to examine their own questions and strug-gles in the modern era with challenges of secularism, technology, mate-rialism, and other religions and philosophies. Christianity may have opportunities to relate to Muslims in transitional and troublesome times. It must be ready for the following:

- Muslim scholars using the historical critical method in studying the perfect Quran
- Muslims considering the issue of freedom of religion and human rights both individually and corporately
- The seeking of spirituality in the crises of faith and in the rise of secularism and materialism

- ✠ The rise of folk Islamic expressions for the need of personal religion, of a relationship with God who responds to the heart, of One like Jesus (Isa) who forgives sins upon confession and who is the Savior who reconciles and who is the Lord whom one can follow and obey

- ✠ Christian wisdom and creativity to relate to Muslims individually and to Muslim people groups across various divides both politically and geographically and culturally.

- ✠ Christian sensitivities and guidance to Muslim converts in their search to live the Christian life within biblical and church norms as well as their cultural backgrounds.

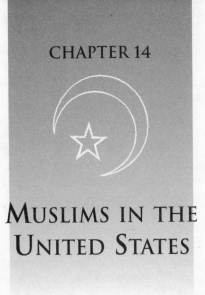

CHAPTER 14

MUSLIMS IN THE UNITED STATES

THE WAVES OF MUSLIMS

The history of Islam in the United States is over two hundred years old.[1] Early records indicate that Arabic-speaking slaves refrained from eating pork in the early 1700s. It is estimated that a fifth of all slaves brought to America during the eighteenth and nineteenth centuries were Muslim. Many of them, however, converted to Christianity.

By 1875, Muslims were migrating to the United States from Syria and Lebanon. The demise of the Ottoman Empire encouraged people to look to the Western nations for work and new opportunities to raise their families.

Larger numbers came especially from the Middle East between World Wars I and II. Many were attracted to Michigan to work in the automobile industry. Mosques were built, and Dearborn began to look like an Arab-Muslim town with its businesses and restaurants.

An even larger group entered the United States between World War II and the mid-1960s. The Middle East and Eastern Europe were undergoing transition, and many fled from political oppression and economic decline. Many were highly educated and wealthy; they settled in various cities.

From the 1970s on, a flood of Muslim immigrants came. They were educated, more westernized, and fluent in English. New oil wealth in the Middle East caused vast development, especially in the rich Muslim countries. They sent their people by the tens of thousands to the United States for education and technical training. Muslim men married American wives. Many remained to raise their families.

Perhaps the largest number of Muslims are from the African-American communities. In the 1930s, Elijah Muhammad, born of a Baptist family in the South, migrated to Detroit, where he met a Muslim named W. D. Fard. From that relationship the Nation of Islam was begun. It has seen many transitions, including the leadership of Wallace D. Muhammad, Malcolm X, and Louis Farrakhan.

Islam is a vibrant and growing religion across the United States. There are thousands of mosques and Islamic associations. Tens of thousands of students from Muslim lands are enrolled in universities. There are estimates of over five million Muslims across the land. Islam is rapidly becoming the second-largest religion behind Christianity, surpassing Judaism.

MUSLIMS OF MANY VARIETIES

Islam has had a colorful history in the United States. Among immigrant-citizens, many associations have been formed. Many gather according to ethnic, linguistic, and national origins. For example, Sunnis and Shiites usually worship in separate locations.

Among the nativistic African-Americans, there have been challenges of keeping the orthodoxy of Islam versus syncretism with other ideologies and traditions. For example, Louis Farrakhan split with Wallace D. Muhammad over the issues of orthodoxy and control. A key matter has been race. Farrakhan continued the racist ideas of Elijah Muhammad while Wallace Muhammad returned to the nonracist teachings of the Quran.

A brief overview of Islamic groups follows:

Moorish Science Temple of America

Noble Drew Ali, born Timothy Drew in rural North Carolina in 1866, founded the Moorish Science Temple of America in 1913 in Newark, New Jersey. He taught that blacks were not of Ethiopian origin but were Moors with Islam as their religion, descendants of the Moabities of Canaan with their homeland in Morocco. Drew used Islam as a way to unite blacks. Jesus was a black man who was executed by the Romans while attempting to redeem the black Moabites.

Some of the leaders exploited the followers by selling relics, magical charms, Old Moorish Healing Oil, and Moorish Purifier Bath Compound. Ali intervened to prevent these practices, and eventually he was mysteriously killed. His death has remained unresolved. Upon his death several factions emerged. Temples have continued in several cities. Some Moors were early converts to the Nation of Islam.

The Ahmadiyya Community of North America

Mirza Ghulam Ahmad founded the Ahmadiyya movement in India. In 1889 he proclaimed himself as the Mahdi whom the prophet Muhammad foretold would come toward the end of the world. His mission was to purify Islam and to convert the world.

Dr. Mufti Muhammad Sadiq established the Ahmadiyya community in the United States in 1921. His initial mission was to convert Islamic immigrants, but he found good response among the African-Americans. The first mosque was built in Chicago. A major practice is *purda*, the separation of women from men, and the women's wearing of the headcovering and face veil. They distribute their own version of the Quran and aggressively seek converts.

Orthodox Islam considers the movement heretical. The Muslim World League has criticized it as a germ in the body of true believers. The League points out its apostasy in that the founder is considered a prophet, that they teach the second coming of Jesus, that the birthplace of Ahmad is a pilgrim site, and that they teach that jihad is un-Islamic.

The American Druze Society

Al-Hakim founded the Druze in Egypt in the eleventh century with roots in Islam. It is a secret society, keeping its beliefs and practices from nonmembers. The Druze first came to the United States from the Middle East in the 1870s. Its headquarters is in Troy, Michigan, and estimates are that there are some five thousand Druze.

Nation of Islam

The Nation of Islam, whose followers were called "black Muslims" by the media, began in the 1930s under the leadership of W. D. Fard and Elijah Muhammad. Elijah, a Baptist from the southern United States, met W. D. Fard in Detroit. Fard, whose origins remain a mystery, taught Elijah a syncretized Islam with mixtures of Christianity, the occult, and racist ideology. Elijah founded the Nation of Islam and established its mosque and headquarters in Chicago. By the time of his death in 1975, the Nation had several million followers with many mosques and land holdings across the United States.

Controversies plagued the Nation of Islam through the 1960s and 1970s. Malcolm X challenged the leadership of Elijah and was consequently assassinated in 1965. Elijah's son, Wallace, criticized his father's unorthodox beliefs and ways and was reprimanded several times. Soon after Elijah's death in 1975, Wallace began to reform the Nation to bring it into line with worldwide orthodoxy.

Louis Farrakhan, who had served under Elijah, broke with Wallace and continued the Nation of Islam along its original path. Wallace formed several associations including The World Community of Islam in the West and the American Muslim Mission. By the early 1980s Wallace had decentralized the American Muslim Mission and had become the titular head of the orthodox Muslims in America.

Ansaru Allah

The Ansaru Allah movement was begun by Isa Muhammad, an African-American, in 1970 in Brooklyn, New York. He had been influenced by the Moorish Science Temple and the Nation of Islam. However, he criticized some of their assumptions and launched his own Islamic movement as a corrective to them.

Other Muslim groups have attacked his authority as an interpreter of the Quran, especially his teaching that women do not have spirits. There are several hundred followers.

The Nubian Islamic Hebrews

The Nubian Islamic Hebrews was begun by Muhammad Ahmed ibn Abd'ullah in New York City in 1970. His followers believe him to be the successor to the prophet Muhammad. Their major belief is that the Nubian (black) race goes back to Adam and Eve. From Abraham there came two nations, namely, the Ishmaelites and the Israelites. Just as the Israelites were held in bondage in Egypt, so the Ishmaelites were in bondage in America for four hundred years. The Nubians came from this bondage.

The American Nubians consider themselves Hebrews. Their theology is a mixture of Jewish, Christian, and Muslim beliefs.

The Hanafi

In 1958 Hamaas Abdul Khaalis (Ernest T. McGee) broke with the Nation of Islam and Elijah Muhammad's teachings and founded The Hanafi movement based in Washington, D.C. He had joined the Nation of Islam in 1950, hoping to bring it in line with orthodoxy.

In 1973 five members of the Nation of Islam murdered seven members of the Hanafi, including five of Khaalis's immediate family. In 1977 members of the Hanafi attempted to stop the screening of the film *Muhammad Messenger of God* by seizing the District of Columbia

Building, the Islamic Center, and the B'nai B'rith Building. They killed one person and took one hundred hostages.

Khaalis was sentenced to prison. His members continue to follow the basic tenets of Sunni Islam and have great hostility toward the Nation of Islam.

The Islamic Party of North America

The Islamic Party of North America was founded in 1972 in Washington, D.C., at the Masjid-al-Ummah. Its purpose is to propagate Islam, and it publishes *al-Islam* which is distributed internationally. Their services include counseling, food distribution to the poor, and properly slaughtered meat (*halal*) at fair prices.

United Submitters International

Rashad Khalifa, an Egyptian, came to the United States in 1959. He obtained a doctorate in biochemistry, married, became a citizen, and presided for eleven years over the mosque in Tucson, Arizona, where he founded United Submitters International.

On January 31, 1990, he was stabbed to death in the mosque by an unknown assailant who has never been apprehended. He used computer analysis to explain the Quran and determined that the number nineteen was the key to interpret it. He taught his followers that he was God's messenger in succession to Abraham and Muhammad.

He attacked Muslims in general and Arab Muslims in particular for their idolatry of following their traditions and not his interpretations. His movement has continued in Arizona in the dissemination of his teachings.

The Federation of Islamic Associations (FIA)

The Federation of Islamic Associations was formed in 1954 "to promote and teach the spirit, ethics, philosophy, and culture of Islam." It publishes the *Muslim Star* and is vigilant against anti-Arab and anti-Islamic media.

The Muslim World League

The Muslim World League was founded in 1962 in Mecca, Saudi Arabia. It is an international organization with an office in New York City. The League has many programs, including the distribution of Islamic materials, financial assistance to Muslims and mosques, and assistance to Muslims in prisons.

The Muslim Student Association (MSA)

The Muslim Student Association began in 1963 with the initiative of Saudi Arabia to counter the Arab Student Organization supported by the Nasser regime of Egypt. It is considered the largest and most active Muslim group in the United States with thousands of Muslim students.

Its monthly journal, *Islamic Horizons,* states the purpose of the Association: "The advancement of unity among Muslims . . . conveying the message of Islam to non-Muslims and removing misconceptions about it and . . . working with Muslims and non-Muslims to address common concerns to improve the quality of life for all."

Many alumni of MSA who have settled in the United States have formed three professional organizations: the Islamic Medical Association, the Association of Muslim Social Scientists, and the Association of Muslim Scientists and Engineers.

The Islamic Society of North America (ISNA)

The Islamic Society of North America was formed in 1982 to meet the needs of Muslim students and Muslim American citizens. One of its major objectives is "to advance the cause of Islam and Muslims in North America." The Muslim Student Association now functions as an agency of ISNA.

The Council of the Masajid

The Council of Masajid operates out of the Muslim World League office in New York City. It promotes cooperation among mosques across the United States as well as internationally. It gives counsel on constructing and maintaining mosques.

The American Muslim Council (AMC)

The American Muslim Council was begun in 1990 with the purpose of "filling a void and providing an indispensable service to the American-Muslim community." It further states, "The American-Muslim community is not an alien community. It is part and parcel of mainstream America. The notion that the moral principles in the United States are based on the Judeo-Christian teachings is inaccurate. More precisely, it is based on the Judeo-Christian-Muslim teachings."

The AMC calls on Muslims to join the council to "ensure that the American-Muslim community is recognized as a constructive force in the political life of this country." The AMC set up a legal department in 1992 to handle cases concerning issues such as child custody, religious rights, and hate crimes against Muslims.

Other goals include setting up a Muslim-American Bar Association, seeking official recognition of major Muslim holidays, and encouraging the United States Postal Service to issue commemorative stamps for the Id Adhan (Abraham's offering of his son) and Id Fitr (the end of the month of fasting). The AMC has also counseled Muslims to join other organizations to request the United States Supreme Court to uphold the ban on assisted suicide.

The American Muslim Alliance (AMA)

The headquarters of The American Muslim Alliance is in Fremont, California, and it has chapters in over thirty states. A major objective of AMA is to "produce qualified Muslim candidates for the political mainstream, and to promote the humanitarian aspect of Islam in this country." A motto has been "2000 for 2000," to have two thousand qualified Muslim candidates running for political office by the year 2000.

MUSLIM PERSONALITIES AND PATTERNS

Orthodox Islam in America follows the basic tenets and practices of orthodox Muslims worldwide. The core beliefs are one God, prophets, angels, scriptures, and the judgment day. The pillars or practices are confession of one God and the last prophet Muhammad, almsgiving, five daily prayers, the month of fasting, the pilgrimage to Mecca, and jihad or mission for God.

The mosque is a place of prayer and worship, usually simple in structure. The imam is the prayer leader who also may have other roles as teacher of the Quran, administrator, and counselor. Friday is the special day of prayer and sermon when Muslims gather at the mosque around noon. They come together for prayer and other meetings at the mosque during the week, but Friday is the high day of gathering.

There are over five million Muslims in the United States. Native-born African-Americans number about half of the total. American Muslims are estimated to be 42 percent African-American; 24.4 percent Asian Indian; 12.4 percent Arab; 5.2 percent African; 3.6 percent Persian; 2.4 percent Turk; 2 percent South Asian; 1.6 percent American white; and 5.6 percent other.

Immigrant Muslims, many of whom have become citizens, have brought their families or have married American spouses who have converted to Islam. They have built their mosques and have followed the essentials of orthodoxy. African-Americans have experienced a mixed history of deviations from orthodoxy, especially under Elijah Muhammad and Louis Farrakhan. Wallace Muhammad has become the titular head of orthodox Islam in America as he reformed the unorthodoxy of his father's movement.

The development of Islam among black Americans may be seen primarily in the leadership of Elijah Muhammad, Malcolm X, Wallace Muhammad, and Louis Farrakhan. Islam among the immigrant Muslims has many leaders, including many of those of the Islamic organizations listed above, and many local imams who preside over group prayers, deliver sermons, and administer mosque affairs voluntarily. Some mosques in the United States are large enough to employ full-time imams.

Mosque on Fourth Street, Washington, D.C., built in the 1950s by Elijah Muhammad, founder of the Nation of Islam. Author and his students talk with the imam of the mosque.

Elijah Muhammad

A movement began in America in the 1930s which would widely appeal to American blacks and which the mass media would label as "black Muslims." Under the banner of Islam it became a movement based on racial purity and segregation. Its leaders became cultic figures.

Elijah Muhammad, born Elijah Poole to a Baptist preacher in Georgia in 1897, moved to Detroit in 1923 with his wife Clara looking for work. He met W. D. Fard, who introduced him to the fledgling organization known as the "Lost-Found Nation of Islam in the Wilderness of North America."

He became Fard's chief minister of Islam and assisted him in building the first temple in Detroit. Upon Fard's death in 1934, Elijah assumed leadership, changed the movement's name to Nation of Islam, and moved its headquarters to Chicago.

Elijah continued the Nation of Islam based on Fard's teachings. Elijah deified Fard as Allah and named himself as the Messenger and Prophet of Allah. "Yacub's History" became the basic narrative for the movement. This narrative taught that original humanity was the black race, that its religion was Islam, and that it founded Mecca. Yacub was the black God who not only created the black race but also the white race.

The white race, a race of devils, ascended to power. God was to reappear, destroy the white race, and restore the black race to its rightful place. Thus, W. D. Fard appeared as God to begin this process.

The Nation of Islam was composed of several organizations. The University of Islam included elementary and secondary schools. The Training and General Civilization Class taught women cooking and sewing. The Fruit of Islam taught men the arts of defense and security and served as bodyguards of Elijah and security agents at all events.

A lifestyle was demanded of hygiene of body and neatness of clothing. Prohibitions included alcohol, narcotics, tobacco, gambling, extramarital sex, and the eating of pork. Members were encouraged to open businesses and buy from one another.

Some tracts of land and buildings were purchased. Elijah called for a separate nation for blacks. Although he used the name Islam, he encouraged little learning of Arabic, built temples instead of mosques, and mixed his ideology and practice with Christianity, Islam, the occult, and racism.

Elijah Muhammad died on February 25, 1975, having led the Nation of Islam for forty-one years. He had amassed tens of thousands of African-Americans together for a fresh identity and for a continuing hope of self-esteem and self-improvement. However, worldwide orthodox Islam gave him no recognition as a leader of Islam, condemned him, and considered his movement a heresy.

He was to leave a legacy of corruption, deception, and financial chaos. His extramarital affairs were to seal his fate in his relations earlier with Malcolm X and later with his son, Wallace. Wallace succeeded his father and eventually led many former followers of The Nation into orthodoxy. Elijah's chief associate, Louis Farrakhan, assembled his hardcore followers and continued the Nation of Islam.

Malcolm X

Malcolm Little was born in Omaha, Nebraska, in 1925, the son of a black Baptist minister. His family was harassed by the Ku Klux Klan, and his home was burned down when he was four. Orphaned at thirteen, he went to live with his sister in Boston.

His early life was involved with drugs, prostitution, and burglary. While serving a six-year prison term, he became a Muslim in 1948. Returning to Detroit, he changed his name to Malcolm X. By 1954, Elijah Muhammad had appointed him minister at the prestigious Harlem Temple No. 7.

Malcolm X gave himself to complete obedience and devotion to Elijah. In 1963 Elijah appointed him the first national minister of the Nation of Islam. He traveled the country speaking before university audiences and on television. However, tensions developed between the two. Malcolm journeyed to Mecca for the pilgrimage, and in his travels and associations with orthodox Muslims, he discovered discrepancies in what Elijah had been teaching about Islam. He also learned of the adulterous life of Elijah.

At the assassination of President John Kennedy, Malcolm said that it was a case of "the chickens coming home to roost." Elijah suspended him from his post. By early 1964, Malcolm left the Nation of Islam, changed his name to El-Hajj Malik El Shabazz, and formed the Organization of Afro-American Unity. He desired to unite blacks and then black-white coalitions would follow.

The Nation of Islam vilified Malcolm, calling him "the worst hypocrite Islam has produced" and "a traitor." He became the target of many threats. On February 21, 1965, as he spoke to members of his organization in Harlem's Audubon Auditorium, he was fatally shot. His three assassins were identified as former members of the Nation of Islam. A week earlier Malcolm had said that there was no better prepared group in the nation to carry out a threat against him than "the Black Muslims." He said he knew because he had taught them himself.

Wallace Deen Muhammad

Upon his father's death in 1975, Wallace became the leader of the Nation of Islam. He was born in 1933 in Michigan but grew up in Chicago. His father had appointed him to many positions, including minister of the temple in Philadelphia, which Malcolm X had begun. He had served time in prison from October 1961 to January 1963 for refusing to report for military service.

Wallace had been suspended from the Nation of Islam by his father several times. In 1964 he accused his father of deception and immorality and was especially tormented by Elijah's infidelities and paternity suits.

His vision was to reinterpret his father's teachings and to introduce orthodox Islam among his followers. He honored the memory of his father by calling Elijah's work the First Resurrection of mental, moral, and physical renewal for blacks. His own work was to be the Second Resurrection.

He established his own teachings and organizational changes. He did not emphasize color, racism, and Yacob's History. God was Divine Mind, not Fard Muhammad, nor black. Wallace taught that Christianity and the church gave birth to the white-devil mentality. He said that the church presented Jesus Christ on the cross as a white god and thus kept black people in oppression.

By late 1976 he changed the name of the Nation of Islam to the World Community of Islam in the West. Its mission was to restore pure Islam while turning to the Quran for truth. Islamic institutions and practices received attention. A temple became a mosque. Chairs were removed and worshipers sat on the floor. A minister became an imam. Members were taught the orthodox forms of prayer and learned the Arabic language to say their prayers.

The Fruit of Islam was disbanded. The name of the University of Islam was changed to the Sister Clara Muhammad Elementary and Secondary Schools. Clara was the name of Wallace's mother. Each mosque became a center of religious and social activities. Wallace formed the Committee to Remove All Images of the Divine, an attempt to remove all displays of pictures and crosses in their religious life.

In April 1980 the name of the organization was changed to the American Muslim Mission. Wallace had increasingly Americanized his movement with displays of the American flag and the pledging of allegiance in his schools. He praised the efforts in the civil rights movement and encouraged the members to become involved. He also changed his name to Warith, meaning "inheritor," and was called imam and president.

Although Wallace had turned his movement toward orthodoxy, many troubles existed. He hailed himself as in the line of the prophets, and an oath of allegiance was given to him and then to the program. Dissension emerged within the leadership of the various imams in the scattered mosques across the country. Louis Farrakhan, whom Wallace had named as imam of the mosque in Chicago, was accused of fomenting trouble. Great financial difficulty faced the American Muslim

Mission when lawsuits were brought against it by the illegitimate children of Elijah.

By 1985 Wallace closed out the American Muslim Mission and integrated it into the general Muslim community in the United States. Its members now are simply called Muslims.

Wallace himself has been given the status as titular head of Muslims in America and has been recognized by worldwide Muslims as an orthodox leader of Islam. He is authorized to grant permission for American Muslims to make the annual pilgrimage to Mecca. He also acts as a trustee for several Muslim nations that fund missionary activities in the United States through the building of mosques and the spreading of Islamic literature.

In the United States he has lectured at universities and churches and synagogues. The United States Senate invited him to give the invocation to open a session in which he prayed to Allah "the Most Merciful Benefactor, the Merciful Redeemer." He has addressed the military leaders at the Pentagon.

Warith D. Muhammad has come full circle from his father's Nation of Islam to become the American leader of Islam respected by both international Muslims as well as domestic politicians. Perhaps one might say that he has begun his third resurrection. Meanwhile, Louis Farrakhan, who left Wallace's movement and leadership in 1978, has continued the tradition of Elijah Muhammad's Nation of Islam.

Louis Farrakhan

Louis Farrakhan's rise to prominence began in the 1960s under the grooming of Elijah Muhammad. He was born in the Bronx in New York City in 1933 but grew up in Boston. Active in the Episcopal Church, he was also a standout student in studies and athletics. He attended Winston-Salem Teachers College. While he was a singer and an accomplished violinist, he met Elijah Muhammad in 1955 and became active in the Nation of Islam.

After joining the Nation of Islam, he changed his name to Louis X. Elijah named him to several posts, including head of the Fruit of Islam, the security force, and minister of the Boston temple. When Malcolm X was murdered in 1965, Elijah appointed him to succeed Malcolm as national representative of the Nation of Islam and as minister of Malcolm's former temple in Harlem. Farrakhan represented Elijah throughout the Nation of Islam until Elijah's death in 1975.

Prior to Elijah's death there had been speculation that Farrakahn would succeed his leader and mentor to whom he had given total obedience and whose views he had represented so well. However, Wallace assumed his father's mantel. As Farrakhan continued to be the charismatic spokesman for the Nation, Wallace reassigned him from the temple in New York to the temple in Chicago. Rumors surfaced of a power struggle between the two.

By March 1978, Farrakhan publicly stated that he was ready to rebuild the Nation of Islam in line with the doctrine of the late Elijah Muhammad. He rejected Wallace's emerging new approach toward Islamic orthodoxy and his reconciliation with whites.

Farrakhan viewed the changes under Wallace as undermining the ability of the Nation of Islam, weakening its effectiveness, and disgracing Elijah Muhammad. He continued the teachings of Elijah on the nature of God, Yacub's History, and the white man as a devil. The newspaper *The Final Call* was resurrected with the format as initiated under Elijah in 1933. The claim has been made that it has the largest circulation of any black periodical in the United States.

Some of the members of the movements under Elijah and Wallace who had dropped out returned to the renewed Nation of Islam. Some brought new recruits. Farrakhan purchased the showcase mosque of Elijah's time in Chicago, refurbished it, and renamed it Maryam Mosque after the mother of Jesus.

He focused much attention on cleanup campaigns in black neighborhoods which included counseling programs for drug addicts, alcoholics, and street gang members. Young men in the Fruit of Islam patrolled the streets of ghettos to ward off drug sellers and users.

Three events propelled Farrakahn into the national spotlight in 1995. He called for, organized, and led "The Million Man March" in Washington, D.C., on October 6. Its stated purpose was to inspire a moral and spiritual rebirth among African-American males. Estimates of the participants ranged from 400, 000 to 860,000.

Also, there was the arrest of Qubilah Shabazz, the daughter of Malcolm X, who was accused of plotting to kill Farrakhan in retaliation for what she believed was his role in her father's murder. And Farrakhan sent members of the Fruit of Islam to California to provide security for the attorneys in the murder trial of O. J. Simpson.

Controversy has followed Farrakhan on his views and speeches on race, black separatism, and anti-Semitism. He and Wallace Muhammad have gone their separate ways in their appeals to African-Americans and their patterns of Islam. Estimates have been made of some 70,000 to 100,000 followers of the Nation of Islam with over eighty mosques.

Examples of Mosques and Programs

There are hundreds of mosques and Islamic centers across the United States. They vary in shapes and sizes and numbers of participants. The Islamic Center of Washington, D.C., located among the embassies along Massachusetts Avenue, has traditional Middle Eastern architecture and decor. The mosque near Toledo, Ohio, located near the intersection of two major interstate highways, is made of white block

Mosque near Toledo, Ohio, with a thousand paved parking spaces

with rising minarets. It has an ultramodern kitchen and dining hall to feed one thousand and a paved parking lot for one thousand vehicles.

The mosque located on the second floor of the international studies building on the campus of Shaw University, a Baptist school in Raleigh, North Carolina, was built with funds donated by the government of Saudi Arabia. It is named The Mosque of the Late King Khalid Ben Abdul Aziz Al Saud.

The Islamic Center of Raleigh is a two-story brick building across the street from the soccer field of North Carolina State University. Hundreds of Muslims gather for Friday noon prayers and the weekly sermon. An accredited elementary school has begun on the grounds. The imam of the mosque came from Damascus, Syria, with his family and has gained American citizenship.

The Islamic community of Cedar Rapids, Iowa, provides a pattern for the growth of Islam. In the early 1920s, Syrian and Lebanese immigrants rented a building for a mosque with twenty members. After World War II, Muslims from Afghanistan, Albania, Indonesia, Iran, Pakistan, Russia, Senegal, and Turkey joined the community. By 1980 there were over 250 members. They started a "Sunday School" for Quranic studies. The government of Egypt gave monies to build a library and study center. A monthly magazine, *The Voice of Islam,* was begun.

Islamic study programs abound on university campuses. Harvard University received a five-million-dollar grant from Saudi Arabia to start a center for Islamic legal studies. The University of Arkansas was given a twenty-three-million-dollar grant from Saudi Arabia to fund a Middle Eastern studies program to include the study of Islam.

Important Dates of Islam in America

1717	Slaves arrive who speak Arabic, eat no pork, and believe in Allah and Muhammad
1790	Moors live in South Carolina in the 1790s
1850	Muslims introduce camels in the Southwest in 1950s. Hajji Ali remains and becomes prospector in California
1875	Muslim immigrants from Syria and Lebanon
1887	Mohammed Alexander Russel Webb becomes first known American convert to Islam. Encounters Islam in Philippines where he is consul
1919	Muslims immigrate to Michigan seeking work in automobile industry. Dearborn develops into "a Muslim town."
1921	Ahmadiyya movement founded
1925	Moorish Temple of Science begun with Noble Drew Ali
1933	W. D. Fard's Temple of Islam in Detroit
1935	Nation of Islam with Elijah Muhammad headquartered in Chicago
1952	Federal government allows Muslim servicemen to identify their religion as Islam
1954	Federation of Islamic Associations founded
1957	Islamic Center of Washington, D. C., opened
1958	Khalifa Hamas Abdul breaks with Nation of Islam and establishes Hanafi Center
1963	The Muslim Student Association begins
1964	Clarence 13 X expelled from Nation of Islam and forms 5 percent Nation of Islam

1964	Malcolm X and Wallace D. Muhammad expelled from Nation of Islam. Louis Farrakhan replaces Malcolm X as national spokesman
1964	Malcolm X establishes Muslim Mosque, Inc.
1965	Malcolm X assassinated
1969	Wallace D. Muhammad reinstated into Nation of Islam
1970	Ansaru Allah is founded by Isa Muhammad
1970	Nubian Islamic Hebrews established by Muhammad Ahmed Abdullah
1972	The Islamic Party of North America organized
1974	Muslim World League granted nongovernmental status at United Nations
1975	Elijah Muhammad dies
1975	Wallace D. Muhammad assumes leadership of Nation of Islam upon father's death. Wallace changes his name to Warith (Inheritor).
1975	Bilalian Community replaces name of Nation of Islam under Warith Muhammad
1976	Silas Muhammad breaks with Warith D. Muhammad and begins the Lost, Found Nation of Islam
1977	World Community of Islam in the West replaces name of Bilalian Community under Warith Muhammad
1977	Louis Farrakhan breaks with Warith D. Muhammad. Farrakhan reestablishes the original Nation of Islam founded by Elijah Muhammad
1978	John Muhammad breaks with Warith D. Muhammad. Forms Nation of Islam under John Muhammad
1978	Caliph Emanuel Muhammad breaks with Warith D. Muhammad. Forms Nation of Islam under his name
1979	Rashad Khalifa becomes the leader of United Submitters International.
1980	American Muslim Mission replaces name of World Community of Islam in the West. Warith D. Muhammad leads it in direction of orthodox Islam
1982	Islamic Society of North America forms
1983	Islamic College founded in Chicago
1985	American Muslim Mission folds. Wallace moves to California. States his followers to be integrated into orthodox Islam and to be known only as Muslims
1990	American Muslim Council founded
1990	Warith D. Muhammad recognized by leading Muslim nations as titular head of Muslims in America and becomes trustee of funding
1992	Warith D. Muhammad invited to give invocation on floor of United States Senate

THE RAPID GROWTH OF ISLAM INTO THE TWENTY-FIRST CENTURY

Islam has challenged the status of Judaism as the second-largest religion in America following Christianity. The following indicate the rapid growth and influence of Islam in the United States.

- Over five million Muslims
- Several thousand mosques and Islamic centers from coast to coast in cities both large and small
- Organizations for Muslims in the professions of medicine, law, engineering, etc., which give them influence in political and economic activities
- Associations of Muslims with the purpose of conserving Islam among the population and spreading Islam in mission activity
- The recognition and cultivation of Muslims by political leaders with invitations to give invocation to open session of Congress and to celebrate Muslim festivities at the White House
- The support of Muslim nations to Muslim leaders in the United States, to American universities, and to Muslim communities with funds for building mosques, Islamic study centers on campuses, and to spread the Islamic religion among the population
- The appointment of Muslim chaplains in the armed services to minister to the thousands of Muslims
- Education and solicitation of Muslim citizens to vote in all local and national elections and to prepare qualified candidates to run for political offices
- Efforts of Muslim associations to gain recognition in American society for the observance of religious holidays in school and other public calendars as those observed by Jews and Christians
- Efforts of Muslims to gain privileges in the workplace for understanding and release of time for daily prayers and other Islamic requirements such as fasting, pilgrimage, and the wearing of specific clothing, especially for women
- Example of Wallace (Warith) Deen Muhammad, the leading figure of American Muslims, receiving the Walter Reuther Humanities Award and the Four Freedoms Award; of being designated by the governments of Saudi Arabia, Abu Dubai, and Qatar as the only trustee in the United States to distribute funds they provide for the propagation of Islam in America
- American Muslims' dealing with living in a society with guarantees of freedom of religion and separation of the powers of state

and religion with their mandates of Islam in the Quran and in the traditions (*hadith*) of their prophet Muhammad

The continuing encounter of Islam with Christianity with the Muslim view of Christianity as a polytheistic religion and attacks upon the Christian teachings of the Trinity and the crucifixion of Jesus Christ

SELECTED READINGS

Ali, Abdullah Yusef. *The Meaning of the Holy Qur'an: New Edition with Revised Translation and Commentary.* Brentwood, Md.: Amana Corporation, 1989.

Arberry, A. J. *The Koran Interpreted,* 2 vols. New York: MacMillan, 1955.

Braswell, George W. Jr. *Islam: Its Prophet, Peoples, Politics, and Power.* Nashville: Broadman & Holman Publishers, 1996.

———. *To Ride a Magic Carpet.* Nashville: Broadman Press, 1977.

———. "A Mosaic of Mullahs and Mosques: Religion and Politics in Iranian Shiah Islam." Ph.D. diss., The University of North Carolina at Chapel Hill, 1975.

———. "The Twenty-first Century Church and the Islamic World." *Faith and Mission Journal* 11, no. 2 (Spring 1994): 64–80.

Cragg, Kenneth. *Muhammad and the Christian.* Maryknoll: Orbis Books, 1984.

———. *The Call of the Minaret.* New York: Oxford University Press, 1964.

Eerdmans Handbook to the World's Religions. Grand Rapids: Wm. B. Eerdmans Publishing Co., 1982.

Esposito, John L. "Islamic Revivalism." *The Muslim World.* Occasional Paper no. 3, 1985.

Geisler, Norman I., and Abdul Saleeb. *Answering Islam.* Grand Rapids: Baker Books, 1993.

Haddad, Yvonne Y. "A Century of Islam in America." *The Muslim World.* Occasional Paper no. 4, 1986.

Johnstone, Patrick. *Operation World.* Grand Rapids: Zondervan Publishing House, 1993.

Kelsay, John. *Islam and War: A Study in Comparative Ethics, the Gulf War and Beyond.* Louisville: Westminster/John Knox Press, 1993.

Khan, Muhammad Muhsin. *The Translation of the Meanings of Sahih al-Bukhari,* Arabic-English, vols. 1–9. Beirut: Dar al Arabia (P. O. Box 6089), n.d.

Lincoln, C. Eric. *The Black Muslims in America.* Grand Rapids: Wm. B. Eerdmans Publishing Co., 1994.

Livingston, Greg. *Planting Churches in Muslim Cities.* Grand Rapids: Baker Books, 1993.

Miller, Judith. *God Has Ninety-Nine Names: Reporting from a Militant Middle East.* New York: Simon & Schuster, 1996.

Miller, William McElwee. *Ten Muslims Meet Christ.* Grand Rapids: Wm. B. Eerdmans Publishing Co., 1969.

Musk, Bill. *The Unseen Face of Islam.* Great Britain: MARC, 1989.

Nasr, Seyyed Hossein. *Ideals and Realities of Islam.* London: George Allen & Unwin Ltd., 1966.

Parrinder, Geoffrey. *Jesus in the Qur'an.* New York: Oxford University Press, 1977.

Parshall, Phil. *Inside the Community: Understanding Muslims Through Their Traditions.* Grand Rapids: Baker Books, 1994.

———. *New Paths in Muslim Evangelism.* Grand Rapids: Baker, 1980.

Register, Ray. *Dialogue and Interfaith Witness with Muslims.* Kingsport, Tenn.: Moody Books Inc., 1979.

Shorrush, Anis A. *Islam Revealed: A Christian Arab's View of Islam.* Nashville: Thomas Nelson Publishers, 1988.

Swarup, Ram. *Understanding Islam Through Hadis.* Delhi: Voice of India, 1983.

Watt, W. Montgomery. *Muslim-Christian Encounters.* London: Routledge, 1991.

Woodberry, J. Dudley., ed. *Muslims and Christians on the Emmaus Road.* Monrovia: MARC, 1989.

ENDNOTES

Chapter 1

1. Population figures are the United Nations' medium variant figures for mid-1996.
2. E. Van Donzel, *Islamic Desk Reference* (New York: E.J. Brill, 1994), 136.

Chapter 2

1. Emory C. Bogle, *Islam Origin and Belief* (Austin: University of Texas, 1998), 18.
2. Mumtaz Ahmad, ed., *State Politics and Islam* (Indianapolis: American Trust Publications, 1986), 26ff. For a complete reading of the Constitution of Medina, please see Afzel Iqbal, *The Prophet's Diplomacy* (Cape Cod: Claude Stark & Co. 1975), 11–15.
3. Muhammad Muslim Khan, *The Translation of the Meanings of Sahih al-Bukhar, Arabic-English*, vols. 1–9 (Beirut: Dar al-Arabia), Hadith 1:199–200; 7.1.331.
4. Ram Swarup, *Understanding Islam Through Hadis* (Delhi: Voice of India, 1983) xv–xvi, as quoted in Phil Parshall, *Inside the Community* (Grand Rapids: Baker, 1994).

Chapter 3

1. Kenneth Cragg and Speight, *House of Islam* (Belmont: Wadsworth Publishing Company, 1988), 11–12.
2. Seyyed Hossein Nasr, *Ideals and Realities of Islam* (London: George Allen & Unwin LTD, 1966), 61.
3. Khan, Sahih al-Bukhari, Hadith 6:431–432; 60.332.459.

Chapter 4

1. George W. Braswell, Jr., *Islam: Its Prophet, Peoples, Politics, and Power* (Nashville: Broadman & Holman Publishers, 1996), 27. (Please see inset "House of God.")
2. Please see an extended discussion of jihad in Braswell, *Islam*, 142–148.
3. M. Amir Ali, Ph.D., *How to Present Islam: A Rational Approach* (Chicago: The Institute of Islamic Information and Education, 1994), 35. The author refers to the references in the Quran on jihad: 2:218; 4:95; 8:72–74; 9:16, 20, 24; 22:78; 61:11.
4. Kenneth Cragg, *Muhammad and the Christian* (Maryknoll: Orbis Books, 1984), 32.
5. Please see George W. Braswell, Jr., *To Ride a Magic Carpet* (Nashville: Broadman Press, 1977), for the flavor of Muslim life around the mosque.

Chapter 5

1. Please see W. Montgomery Watt, *Muhammad: Prophet and Statesman* (London: Oxford University Press, 1946) for his discussion of these characteristics.
2. Ira G. Zepp, Jr., *A Muslim Primer* (Westminster, Md.: Wakefield Editions, 1992), 197.
3. Please see Judith Miller, *God Has Ninety-Nine Names: Reporting from a Militant Middle East* (New York: Simon & Schuster, 1996), for significant data on the contemporary Middle East and Islamic patterns.

Chapter 6

1. Please refer to George W. Braswell, Jr., *To Ride a Magic Carpet* (Nashville: Broadman Press, 1977) for details of the Shiite ceremonies surrounding the month of Muharram and the events commemorating the death of Husain.
2. Please see George W. Braswell, Jr., *To Ride a Magic Carpet* (Nashville: Broadman Press, 1977) for examples of prayers and shrines in the name of various Shiite heroes illustrative of folk Islam.

Chapter 7

1. Khan, Sahih al-Bukhari, Hadith 5:37.1; 59:37.524.

Chapter 8

1. Abul Fael Mohsin Ebrahim, *Abortion, Birth Control and Surrogate Parenting: An Islamic Perspective* (Indianapolis: American Trust Publications, 1989), 23.
2. D. S. Roberts, *Islam* (New York: Harper and Row Publishers, 1982), 78–79.
3. John Kelsay, *Islam and War: A Comparison in Ethics, the Gulf War and Beyond* (Louisville: Westminster/John Knox Press, 1993), 35–36.
4. W. Montgomery Watt, *Muslim-Christian Encounters* (London: Routledge, 1991), 61–62.
5. Please see Emory C. Bogle, *Islam Origin and Belief* (Austin: University of Texas Press, 1998), for sections on Islam's confrontation with modern secularism.
6. John L. Esposito, "Islamic Revivalism," *The Muslim World Today*, no. 3 (Washington, D.C.: American Institute for Islamic Affairs, 1985), 1.

Chapter 9

1. Martin Luther, *On War Against the Turks*, trans. C. M. Jacobs and R. C. Schultz in Luther's Works, ed. by H. T. Lehmann (Philadelphia: Fortress Press, 1967), 170–77.

Chapter 10

1. Please see Geoffrey Parrinder, *Jesus in the Quran* (New York: Oxford University Press, 1977) for an excellent resource on references to Jesus and Christians as found in the Quran.

Chapter 12

1. Please see William E. Phipps, *Muhammad and Jesus* (New York: The Continuum Publishing Company, 1996), for helpful information comparing various topics on Muhammad and Jesus.

Chapter 14

1. Please see George W. Braswell, Jr., "Muslims in America: A Growing Religion," *Islam: Its Prophet, Peoples, Politics, and Power* (Nashville: Broadman & Holman Publishers, 1996), 207–46 for an in-depth study of Islam in America.